Peter Rutherford

Sinónimos ingleses explicados

English Synonyms Explained

(Differences in Word Use in English)

ENGLISH LANGUAGE BOOKS

ANGLO DIDACTICA

The image used on the cover of this book is from Corel Professional Photos: Abstract Textures CD-ROM.

Impreso en España
Printed in Spain

ISBN: 84-86623-86-3

Depósito legal: M. 1.720-2001

Editorial Anglo Didáctica, S. L.
C/ Santiago de Compostela, 16
28034 Madrid - Spain
Tel.: 91 378 01 88

Impreso por Fareso, S. A.
Paseo de la Dirección, 5 - 28039 Madrid

AL ESTUDIANTE DE INGLES

Al comenzar el estudio de otro idioma, uno de nuestros primeros problemas es aprender el vocabulario inicial. Pero cuando llegamos más allá de esta etapa, empezamos a estar conscientes de lo poco que sabemos. Resulta cada vez más evidente que ese idioma contiene muchas más palabras de las que al principio se esperaba encontrar.

Después se presenta otro problema: que para cada vocablo que buscamos, los diccionarios suelen ofrecer algunos sinónimos, pero a menudo ocurre que el profesor rechaza el que hemos elegido, y no siempre parece saber explicar su motivo. Entonces empezamos a sospechar que en realidad no se trata de auténticos sinónimos. Nos damos cuenta de que puede haber matices significativos de diferencia entre ellos, y esa posiblidad nos preocupa en serio.

Es precisamente por esto que tuve la idea de escribir este libro. Mi experiencia como profesor de inglés me enseñó lo frustrante que es para un alumno realmente interesado, descubrir una serie de palabras con más o menos el mismo significado, sin poder averiguar cuál es la exacta, o al menos, la más apropiada para cada caso.

El propósito de este libro es doble: por un lado, distinguir entre dos o tres voces o frases frecuentemente confundidas, y, por otro, proporcionar al estudiante varias palabras similares a la vez, pero también resaltando las diferencias que hay entre ellas.

De este modo espero ayudarle a aumentar su vocabulario, y lo que es más importante, saber escoger mejor la palabra inglesa que necesita.

El autor.

INTRODUCTION

What is this book for?

To serve as a source of consultation, reference, and vocabulary information for foreign students of English, especially where subtle semantic differences leave the student bewildered.

Why was it written?

Because vocabulary is such a big field of learning; and as English contains so many confusingly similar terms, even the best dictionary can only provide individual meanings, not satisfactory distinctions and comparisons of meaning.

It is also aimed at the hoary problem of composition-writing. Many years of teaching English to foreign students (Spanish in particular), showed me the kind of problems students have to face in writing English. No matter how good their general command of vocabulary, when trying to compose a written text, they keep encountering two principal obstacles: which of two or more words or phrases is the right one for the situation, and, apart from the already familiar words and phrases, what unknown alternatives exist that might well be much more appropriate – and worth learning?

When it is clearly essential to acquire a wider and better vocabulary, we teachers invariably recommend extensive reading, but few students these days can find the necessary time – nor does that advice help when the student is confronted by a sudden and immediate need.

It seemed to me that what was direly lacking was a simple book of quick reference for such contingencies, and that is the void that this book sets out to fill. I also trust that the book will help students not only to extend their range of vocabulary but to feel encouraged to use terms that had previously daunted them.

How is the book organized?

Every word or phrase that causes the student trouble is called a *problem item* (listed under "Contents").

Every problem item has a heading that includes all the confusing words, which is followed by an individual explanation for each word listed. Where the purpose is to offer the reader alternative vocabulary forms to the probably more elementary ones that are already familiar, there is a simple general heading, such as "Ways of walking". And for every item, whenever feasible one or more typical example sentences are provided to illustrate the use and meaning of the word in question.

Furthermore, all the words referred to in the book are listed alphabetically in an Index at the end. Those printed in bold (blacker) lettering are the problem items under which these other words can be found and which, for easy location, appear in alphabetic order throughout the book.

For whom is the book intended?

For intermediate and advanced students, as most of the explanations given require a reasonably good command of English, and although many of the problems covered are relatively elementary in themselves, much of the alternative vocabulary offered is of an advanced level, because this is precisely the area in which it is most needed.

The author.

CONTENTS: LIST OF PROBLEM ITEMS

35 Die, Be killed
36 Differ, Vary
37 Dirty, Grubby, Grimy, Filthy, Foul
38 Door, Gate, Doorway, Gateway
39 Duck, Cower, Cringe, Grovel (all verbs)
40 Earn, Gain, Win
41 Earth, Land, Ground, Soil
42 Economic, Economical
43 End, Ending, Finish
44 Entrance, Entry
45 Famous, Notorious
46 Fatal, Deadly, Deathly, Lethal, Mortal
47 Find, Meet, Encounter, Meet with, Run into, Come across,
    Discover, Locate, Detect
48 Fit, Suit
49 Floor, Storey
50 Full, Sheer, Utter
51 Gather, Collect, Accumulate, Assemble
52 Gold/Golden, Gilt, Silver/Silvery, Lead/Leaden, Brass/Brazen,
    Wood/Wooden, Wool/Woollen
53 Grateful, Gratified, Thankful, Thankless
54 Happy, Unhappy, Sad, Cheerful, Pleased, Glad
55 Hint, Imply, Intimate, Insinuate
56 Historic, Historical
57 Holding with pressure
58 -ic / -ical Endings
59 Just, Only
60 Just (used with tenses)
61 Kind, Kindly
62 Known
63 Last, Latest, Final, Ultimate
64 Laughing, Smiling
65 Lay, Lie
66 Life, Living, Livelihood
67 Light effects
68 Like, As
69 Liquid movement

70 Little, Small
71 Looking (Ways of Looking)
72 Loudness of voice
73 Matter, Affair, Issue, Problem, Subject, Theme, Topic
74 Mischievous, Malicious, Spiteful, Vicious
75 North, Northern, Northerly
76 Obvious, Evident, Apparent, Patent, Blatant
77 Occasion, Opportunity, Chance
78 Pay, Pay for
79 Plague, Pest, Blight
80 Plenty, Full
81 Polite, Courteous, Civil
82 Port, Harbour, Haven
83 Posture
84 Preoccupy, Worry
85 Preserve, Conserve
86 Private, Intimate, Intimacy, To intimate, Intimation
87 Product, Produce
88 Pulling (Ways of Pulling)
89 Pushing (Ways of Pushing)
90 Quick, Fast, Rapid, Swift
91 Rather than
92 Reach, Attain, Achieve, Obtain
93 Realize, Notice
94 Relation, Relations, Relationship
95 Rent, Hire, Lease, Charter
96 Road, Roadway, Street
97 Rob, Steal
98 Running, Jumping
99 Scoff, Mock, Jeer, Tease, Taunt
100 Seeing (Ways of Seeing)
101 Shade, Shady, Shadow, Shadowy
102 Shape, Form
103 Ship, Boat, Craft, Vessel
104 Shoot, Fire, Aim, Hit, Miss
105 Sign, Signal
106 Sincere, Honest, Truthful, Candid, Frank

107 Soon, Quickly
108 Special, Especial, Specially, Especially
109 Substitute, Replace
110 Sure, Safe, Secure
111 Sure (to), Certain (to), Bound to
112 Sympathy, Compassion, Pity
113 Taking (Ways of taking what is not yours)
114 Tall, High, Low, Height, Tallness
115 Town, Country, Countryside, Landscape
116 Trouble, To trouble, Nuisance, Bother
117 Undoubtedly, Without doubt, Doubtless, No doubt, I'm sure
118 Unexpected applications (familiar words used in unexpected ways)
119 View, Viewpoint, Opinion, Attitude, Outlook, Manner, Behaviour
120 Wait, Expect, Hope
121 Walking (Ways of Walking)
122 Wall, Fence, Hedge, Railing(s)
123 Wander, Roam, Rove, Stray
124 Want, Wish, Desire
125 Willing, Prepared, Ready, Keen, Eager
126 Worth, Worth while, Worthwhile, Worthy
127 Wreck, Wreckage, Shipwreck

1 ABLE ~ CAPABLE

1. Used attributively (that is, before a noun describing some kind of person), both **able** and **capable** describe that person's *competence in doing things*:

    > *Alice was the ablest/most capable cook they had ever known; her repertoire ranged from simple day-to-day cooking to the most splendid of "cordon bleu" dishes, and she could cook for any number of diners.*

2. But there are complications when these adjectives are used after the verb "to be": that is, structurally –when they affect the meaning of the whole sentence, not of just one noun.

Let's look at the structures first:

able (and its negative, **unable**) is always followed by *to* with an *infinitive verb*;

capable (like the negative **incapable**) is followed by *of* plus a *noun* or *gerund*.

Able to

This adjective indicates two things:

a) that what happens is *either because of certain physical qualities or because of favourable circumstances* (here, we could also use the verb "can");

b) that it happens only *on one particular occasion*, not several, and not over a period of time. ("Can" does not have this special meaning.)

    > *By inserting something like a nail file, a child would be able to prise this medicine bottle open.*
    > This is an imaginary case in which a child's known skill at manipulating the nail file – a *physical quality* – would make it possible to open the bottle. This, or some similar action, has very likely already happened at some time.

    > *We were able to see the summit of the mountain that day, because for once there was no cloud to hide it.*
    > In this case it was the absence of cloud – *exceptionally favourable circumstances* – that made it possible to see the top of the mountain.

If insects were not restricted by the limitations of their breathing system, which, being a network of minute tubes that extends throughout the body, becomes less efficient the longer it is, they might be able to achieve the terrifying sizes that fantasy films love to portray.

This is a case that is valid for all insects and at all times.

Capable of

In contrast to the above, **capable of** tells us that a certain thing or situation *may* happen, and at any time, but not that it actually happens. In describing people, it often warns us of an unexpected reaction to circumstances or tells us of a hidden, and thus a surprising, quality of character:

Spider's silk is capable of bearing strains that would break any similar thread made of metal.

This does not tell us that spider's silk *does* bear such strain but merely that this is a possibility.

Despite his age, my grandfather was capable of amazing feats of agility.

Evidently the old gentleman had demonstrated these feats on more than one occasion, but they were not habitual in him.

The Romans were justly famous for civilising Europe, yet they were capable of appalling cruelty.

We know of many instances of this cruelty, but it does not make us think badly, on the whole, of the Romans.

2 ABOVE ~ OVER ~ BELOW ~ UNDER ~ BENEATH ~ UNDERNEATH

Over and **under** are easy to understand when they mean movement, but all of these six prepositions can be difficult to distinguish when they are used to show static physical position. Let's look first at **above** and **over**, which refer to upper positions.

Above

This is the word to use when one thing is situated higher – especially *directly higher* – than another, and when there is *no contact* between the two things being compared. There may indeed be a certain distance separating them, but a vertical line drawn upwards from the lower thing would reach the higher one exactly. In the human face, for example, *the nose is positioned above the mouth.*

Below

This is the exact opposite of **above**, so (to continue the former example) *your mouth is below your nose.*

Above and **below** are both used in making *vertical measurements*:

> *The town is only a few metres above sea level, so the humidity is very high there.*
>
> *I looked down from the tower to the valley below me.*

Over

This also means "higher than", but with these differences: *the two things are not necessarily in a vertical plane, there is often contact* between them, and *the upper one in some way covers* the lower and extends a little beyond, which also means that it can protect it. For instance, we lay a tablecloth over the table (to both cover and protect it) or we hold an umbrella over us when it rains. The exact opposite is **under.**

Under

This word indicates a *lower position, usually with contact.* In this sense we talk about the ground under our feet, the veins under our skin, or dirt under our fingernails. However, unlike **over**, it does not mean that the lower object is completely covered:

> *He was lying hopelessly drunk under the table, with his feet on a cushion he had obviously taken from the armchair.*

Both **over** and **under** are used for numbers, especially those that indicate *ages* and *speeds*:

> *Over ten thousand people have visited the museum so far this year.*
>
> *If you are over eighteen and under twenty-five you are eligible for special travel discounts.*
>
> *The vehicle must have been going at well over 200 kilometres per hour to have crashed with such violence.*

Beneath

This is like **below**, in the sense of exact position (and they occupy the same area), but the two things, although not in direct contact and there is no idea of covering, are *very near each other*:

> *The excavators found the remains of a prehistoric altar beneath the church foundations, proving that the church had been built on a much earlier, pagan site.*

Underneath

As the form of the word shows, this is an extended version of **under**, so the notion of covering is important: the lower object is *hidden and therefore protected*:

> *Hearing a strange noise from the rubbish heap, I bent down to look and saw two little children huddled underneath a large sheet of dirty cardboard.*

3 ACT ~ ACTION

It is convenient to present these in reverse order.

Action

1. Any *movement* that results in some kind of change –a change of position, for example, or of circumstances:

> *The government's belated action in introducing an antiterrorist law met with only qualified approval from the public.*

2. In military terms, **action** (here uncountable) is any kind of *offensive operation* against the enemy:

> *As the bombers appeared in the sky, the local anti-aircraft guns came into action.*

Act

1. This is an action *made in public* (and often premeditated) that has significant consequences or that clearly demonstrates a feeling or attitude:

> *The new ruler's first act was to proclaim freedom of speech.*

> *Any press criticism of police behaviour is interpreted as an act of defiance against the regime and severely punished.*

2. Legally, it means *a record of what has been discussed and decided*, as in a meeting or council:

    > *All decisions made here are recorded in our Book of Acts.*
    >
    > *An Act of Parliament has the force of law in this country.*

3. A third meaning is *a division of a play or opera*:

    > *Carmen's importance in the plot grows with each of the opera's three acts.*

4. The verb **to act** means either *to perform in the theatre (or as if in a theatre)* or *to do something that will produce results*:

    > *That frown on her face doesn't mean anything, you know; she's only acting!*
    >
    > *The king decided to act before the conspirators had time to complete their plans, and they were all arrested.*

4 AFRAID TO ~ AFRAID OF

Afraid means *suffering fear*, and in its simplest sense we often come across the confession that somebody is **afraid of** something horrible or frightening, like snakes or spiders or lightning. But it is when the above phrases are followed by a verb that complications arise.

Afraid to

This is always followed by the infinitive of a verb, the kind of verb that denotes action. The complete phrase tells us what action is intended and that the doer feels fear, but the result is negative – *the proposed action does not take place*, precisely because of the fear:

> *She found herself standing next to Anthony Hopkins at one of these parties, but she was afraid to speak to him and so missed a golden chance of getting his autograph.*
>
> *As the great majority of rape victims are afraid to report their experience to the police, it is only the few brave women who do so whose cases come to light.*

Afraid of

This can be followed by a noun or by a verb of action, which is always in the gerund form. In either case this – like the snakes and the spiders mentioned above – is what causes the fear. In the case of a verb the person is *afraid that if he does the action he will suffer its consequences*, and this thought leaves him irresolute. This doesn't mean that the action itself is unpleasant, but the consequences could be regrettable, and the person knows that. In fact, in many cases the action is something terribly tempting; it is the fear of the results that makes us hesitate:

> *I desperately wanted to give my opinion in the discussion, but I was afraid of being laughed at, so I kept silent.*

5 ALMOST ~ NEARLY

These two adverbs are generally synonyms of each other, but of course there are some differences. The first difference is merely one of register: **almost** is more formal than **nearly**. The second difference is one of meaning: **nearly** implies *progress towards a desirable state*, whilst **almost** is used for *cases of close similarity*. Consequently there are certain occasions when only one can be used. For instance, when the adverb describes an approach to an action, process, or stage of development that, because of natural circumstances, *can never take place*, only **almost** can be used to express it.

Compare these:

1. *I've nearly (almost) finished this, so I'll be ready to come with you in a few minutes.*
   = No difference.

2. *Baby can nearly talk now.*
   We expect all babies to begin to talk sooner or later, and this one is clearly making good progress.

3. *Our dog is so intelligent, you know – he can almost talk!*
   Obviously, the dog will never really talk. To use **nearly** would suggest that if we wait long enough the dog will be able to converse with us!.

4. *Try the face cream I use: you'll find it almost as good as yours.*
   But it will never be just as good.

N.B.   In a similar but *negative situation*, only **nearly** can be used:

You won't find anything nearly as good as this cream.

Unfortunately he wasn't nearly well enough prepared for the job they wanted him to take on and made a mess of it.

But don't put **nearly** before negative words like "nobody" or "never", and although **almost** in this position is sometimes heard, it is far more usual to say "hardly anybody, hardly anything" or "hardly ever":

It (almost never) / hardly ever rains in this country.

6 AMUSING ~ FUNNY ~ FUN ~ ENTERTAINING

Although **amusing** is perhaps the easiest of these words to recognize, it is better to begin the explanations with **funny.**

Funny

This adjective has acquired two very different meanings, in exactly the same way as its counterparts in French (drôle) and German (komisch), so it can now mean either "comical" or "strange, inexplicable", according to the sense of the context:

His performance was so funny that the audience were convulsed from beginning to end.

That's funny: I put my handbag down here only a moment ago, and now it's gone!

Fun

Besides its use as a noun, meaning *a highly enjoyable activity*, this word has developed into an adjective that we use to describe people, things, or actions. Then we mean that we *enjoy the company* of these people or find those things interesting and enjoyable to do:

I like you – you're fun to go out with!

Don't take this ceremony seriously: it's just a fun thing that we do at this time of year.

Amusing

So what about this word? It means *moderately funny: something that makes us smile rather than laugh*:

> *The story was amusing, but not amusing enough to be heard more than once.*

Entertaining

This means *not only amusing but – especially – interesting.* It's a word we use to describe books, films, talks, games, etc. – plus people and activities – that, while being amusing in themselves, keep us interested:

> *He's such an entertaining talker that I could listen to him all night!*

7 ANNOY ~ BOTHER ~ DISTURB ~ MOLEST ~ WORRY

Annoy

Basically, this means *to anger to some extent*, by doing things either at the wrong moment or that are not wanted by the other person at all, or generally by behaving (whether intentionally or not) in a way that the other person dislikes:

> *The children annoyed the old man by knocking at his door and running away when he came to open it.*
>
> *It does annoy me when he switches my television on without even asking me.*

Bother

This refers:

1. To requests or demands, or demanding situations, that mean that someone *has to do something he or she would not normally do at all or would not do at that precise moment*:

> *Please don't bother me with any more pleas to take you to the zoo today, when you know I can't leave the house yet.*
>
> *I thought of phoning you about it, but I guessed you'd be in bed by then, so I didn't bother (to phone).*

2. To recent events or circumstances that *take away our peace of mind*:

> *It bothered her all day that she had omitted to kiss her father when she left him.*

(Also see **Trouble**)

Disturb

1. Disturbing someone means *interrupting them at an inconvenient moment,* such as when they are relaxing or sleeping, or working or trying to concentrate:

> *Notice on hotel bedroom door: "Do not disturb".*
>
> *Don't move, or you'll disturb the mother bird and she'll fly away in fright.*
>
> *Children, try not to disturb the cook while she's making the soufflé: it needs a lot of attention.*

2. Referring to things that happen, it also means *to make someone feel uneasy or unhappy*:

> *We were disturbed to hear that our only son was planning to enter a monastery.*
>
> *It disturbs me to see how many dogs are abandoned when the holiday period starts.*

Molest

This is very similar to **annoy**, in the sense that the victim reacts with anger, but this is often a result of alarm or fright as well. There is frequently a sexual interpretation:

> *A man has been arrested for molesting women on the train.*

Worry

This is a more intense form of **disturb** (2), in which we simply cannot stop thinking about a problem, and this obsession is so great that it prevents us finding a solution:

> *I can see you've been worrying all night about that debt, haven't you? There are dark rings round your eyes.*
>
> *He worried so much about his job that it made him ill.*

(Also see **Preoccupy**)

17

8 ARGUMENT ~ DISCUSSION ~ DEBATE

Argument (verb: to argue)

This can be one of two things:

1. A belief expressed to other people in a way that *tries to convert them to that same belief*:

   The writer of this article presents very persuasive arguments for declaring the old station a national monument.

2. A situation in which each person is interested only in *forcing the others to accept his or her opinion*. Such "conversations" easily become very heated, because no-one wants to listen to anyone else's arguments:

   It was only a light collision, but the two drivers at once jumped out of their cars and began a fierce argument, each accusing the other of driving dangerously.

Discussion (verb: to discuss)

This time the conversation is a serious one, between people who are *ready to modify their own opinions* by listening attentively to the views of the others:

   I learned a lot about the theatre through listening to radio discussions between dramatists and famous actors.

Debate (verb: also, to debate)

This is *an intellectual exercise* in which the participants argue for or against a topic chosen in advance, with a vote at the end. In universities, it constitutes a kind of game that teaches students the value of presenting a serious, balanced argument, even when the topic is a trivial one:

   The debate in Parliament on modifying the immigration laws led to a radical change of attitude on the part of the Opposition.

   The subject of yesterday's debate, competently defended by our side, was whether women would need less make-up if they had to shave.

9 ASPECT ~ APPEARANCE ~ SIGHT ~ PROSPECT

Aspect

This is what we see when we look at something *from different angles or viewpoints*. For instance, buildings have various aspects according to their orientation and to the beholder's position, and each aspect can cause a different emotional response in the beholder: the southern aspect (the one facing the sun in the northern hemisphere) probably strikes him as more cheerful and more colourful, while the northern aspect is likely to seem severe and bleak:

> *Being a painter, he was greatly interested in the northern aspect of the cottage he hoped to buy.*

> *Seen from that new aspect, the problem looked even worse than we had thought at first.*

Appearance

This is how something looks *at different times or in different circumstances*, not from different positions. For example, a tree looks different (has a different appearance) according to the season of year:

> *Covered so thickly with snow, the valley presented an unfamiliar, but delightful, appearance.*

> *We were shocked at the change in his appearance after his illness.*

Sight (of something)

This is more a matter of *the impression made on the beholder* on seeing something than its true appearance when regarded objectively. In other words, what counts is the beholder's reaction to what he sees:

> *The sight of so much blood horrified even so hardened a man as the detective was.*

> *It would be a marvellous sight to see the streets completely void of cars for once.*

> *What a sight she was, with her hair in a mess and her makeup smeared across her face! I had never imagined she could look anything but perfect.*

Prospect

This is literally *what is seen before us,* that is, not only what we are looking at but *what it can mean for us* in the future:

> *The prospect of a lonely old age drives many people to remarry late in life.*

In the plural, **Prospects** refers particularly to *possibilities of improvement in one's work*:

> *What interests me is not the present conditions of the job but the prospects it offers.*

10 ASSASSIN ~ ASSASSINATION ~ MURDER ~ MURDERER ~ KILLER

The legal code defines the crime of killing another person as either **murder, manslaughter** or **homicide**, the precise classification being determined by the circumstances of the crime. So evidently assassination is not included; then what is **assassination** and what is an **assassin**? Let's see...

Assassin

This word originated in the eleventh century, from a secret society in the Middle East whose members killed those they regarded as their enemies while under the influence of the drug hashish, on account of which their name in Arabic was "hashashin" (drinkers of hashish):

> *The film is about a hired assassin who was trying to shoot General de Gaulle at a public ceremony.*

Assassination

Today this term describes the killing of someone, not for personal reasons but for *what that person represents*. Consequently, typical assassination victims are statesmen, politicians, and leaders of religious or idealistic movements. If such a person is killed because of jealousy, say, the crime is considered murder; but if his or her death removes some kind of social obstacle, that is assassination.

Some of the many famous people who have been assassinated are: Julius Caesar (seen as an enemy of the old Roman republic), the Austrian Archduke Franz Ferdinand, and Martin Luther King. Victims of murder are far more numerous, unfortunately, but much less well known, although often their murderers acquire disproportionate notoriety:

> *The case of President Kennedy is still enigmatic: if it is discovered that he was killed for purely personal reasons, this will be another instance of murder, but owing to his great political importance we tend to assume that this was assassination.*

Murder and Murderer

When a case of unlawful killing comes to court, it is frequently found that it was committed intentionally to *benefit the criminal* personally in some way. Then it is defined as **murder**, and its perpetrator is a **murderer**:

> *They say he was murdered by someone in the family who hoped to inherit his fortune.*

> *Statistics show that violent murders are the ones most committed by men, while women prefer subtler methods, such as poisoning.*

Killer

The media, which have a fondness for this term, use it to refer to a murderer who *repeats the action* and is therefore feared by the general public. However, a **killer** can equally well be some animal or species of animal that has a reputation for murderous ferocity, such as sharks:

> *For months the entire city lived in terror of the killer of a number of beautiful girls, fearing the moment when he would strike again.*

11 AVOID ~ PREVENT

Let's begin with **Prevent** because it is easier to recognize:

Prevent

1. This verb means *ensure that something does not happen.* It is a transitive verb, followed by an object that signifies something or some situation that is unwanted or frankly undesirable:

    Careful driving prevents accidents.

    It was only the immediate intervention of the United Nations that prevented a war between the two countries.

    Far too little is being done to prevent the complete destruction of the world's rainforests.

2. It is very often followed by an (indirect) object plus a second verb in the gerund form (usually introduced by "from") to specify *the precise action that now will not take place*:

    Any more heavy rain like today's will prevent the farmers from harvesting the wheat.

    The ministers conferred hastily as to how to prevent the news from becoming public knowledge.

    Her mother's illness prevented Jane from going on holiday.

Avoid

1. Also a transitive verb and with a direct object, this means *proceed, but without contact with something unpleasant or undesirable*:

    I saw the glass in the roadway just in time to avoid it.

    I tried hard to signal to him, but he kept avoiding my eyes.

2. It, too, can be followed by a second, gerundive verb (as with **prevent**, but without an object), and then the meaning is *stop oneself from doing something*:

    The speaker wisely avoided making any reference to the growing tensions within the Party.

If I were in your delicate position, I would avoid committing myself to any course of action at all.

Many film stars try to avoid being recognized in public by wearing dark glasses.

12 BARBARIC ~ BARBAROUS

Both these adjectives derive from "barbarian", the Greek description for non-Greeks and therefore for their outlandish ways, but the Romans' later experience of Germanic tribes gave these words a purely negative meaning – one that reflects the fear or contempt aroused by contact with a supposedly inferior culture.

Barbaric

This word, when correctly used, describes the *external impression* made by what we consider to be uncivilized peoples, in particular the gaudiness of their dress and ornaments, and the wildness of their music. Unfortunately it is often used where **barbarous** is meant:

> *The barbaric attire and ferocious gestures of tribal warriors are calculated to inspire terror in their enemies.*

> *For his opera "Prince Igor", Borodin wrote some particularly dramatic music to represent the barbaric singing and dancing of the Polovtsi people.*

Barbarous

This refers to the uncivilized, and consequently appalling, *behaviour* traditionally ascribed to savages but too often displayed by modern "civilized" societies:

> *Stalin's rule has been widely condemned for the barbarous treatment of ethnic minorities, who were constantly persecuted and, in the event of an uprising, deported or even massacred wholesale.*

13 BARE ~ NAKED ~ NUDE

Bare

Anything, including the body or parts of it, that is *not covered* is **bare**, whether accidentally or by design:

> *Erosion had left the hillside bare of soil.*
>
> *It is dangerous to touch this product with bare hands.*
>
> *I ran out of the bathroom in bare feet to answer the telephone.*

But it can also mean *unadorned* or *without any additions*:

> *The wall looked sadly bare without my posters on it.*
>
> *Please tell us the bare truth and nothing more.*

Naked

For the body, we use this adjective *when those parts that people think should normally be kept covered are not*:

> *A huge wave threw him over, pulling off his swimming shorts and leaving him stark naked.*

But we use the expression "to see something with the **naked** eye" to mean without using any kind of spectacles, while "a **naked** flame" is a flame that is not protected in any way, such as that of a candle.

Nude

This refers exclusively to the human body and also means "unclothed", but *in the artistic sense*, where it is the presentation of the body that counts:

> *Our art class spent the morning drawing a nude girl model.*
>
> *The first nude statue erected in London was the Achilles that stands at the corner of Hyde Park.*

14 BARE ~ UNCOVER ~ DENUDE ~ EXPOSE ~ EXPOUND ~ REVEAL ~ UNEARTH
(all verbs)

Bare or Uncover

When we **bare** or **uncover** something, we remove whatever normally keeps it covered, but the difference is that the things we **bare** are those that *society considers should be kept covered* for reasons of propriety, such as parts of the body, whilst **uncovering** concerns anything that has been *covered only for a certain reason or time*:

> *The peasants bared their heads as the Tsar passed.*
> They normally wore hats all the time and took them off this time only out of respect.

> *When she uncovered the basket, we saw that it was full of strawberries.*

Denude and Expose

Denuding and **exposing** both mean *uncovering some physical object that should be kept covered and thus protected*, but where **denuding** is permanent, **exposing** is temporary:

> *Forest fires had denuded the area of trees.*
> It would take many years for the trees to grow again.

> *When you open the camera shutter the film is momentarily exposed to the light.*

> *Not wearing sunglasses in bright sunshine exposes one's eyes to dangerous ultraviolet rays.*

Expound

This verb is used only *for expressing ideas in detail*:

> *He expounded his theory to an assembly of the nation's leading scientists.*

Reveal

We **reveal** anything that has been *kept secret* until now:

> *She was finally induced to reveal her motive for stealing the money.*

25

Press reports reveal that the minister had known all about the corruption from the start and had kept silent.

Unearth

This means *digging up* something that was buried: (literally, that was under the earth):

While digging in the garden I unearthed part of the well that had once supplied the cottage with all its water.

But it can be used effectively instead of **reveal** when *the secret had previously been very well guarded*:

Police inquiries unearthed a plot to assassinate the president.

15 BEACH ~ BANK ~ SHORE ~ SEASIDE ~ STRAND ~ COAST

Beach

The characteristics of a beach are these:

- It is an area of land alongside water, especially the sea.
- It is a more or less flat area, although it may be interrupted by stones or rocks.
- It is a suitable place for landing from a small boat or pulling it out of the water.
- If it is composed of sand, it may soon become popular as a bathing spot:

  We spent the afternoon sunbathing on the quieter of the town's two beaches.

Bank

This one of the two sides of a long, narrow stretch of water such as a river or canal:

Let's go for a walk along the canal bank until dinnertime.

Shore

Essentially the place where land meets a lake or the sea; in a stricter sense it is *that part of land onto which one can step from a boat*. In this connection we have phrases like "to go or to be ashore" and "to be on shore", which mean having left the water. A shore may be formed of sand, mud, shingle, or small rocks, but not large rocks or cliffs:

> *The shore we were approaching was rocky and did not at first look suitable for unloading our cargo.*

Seaside

This is basically an area of land beside the sea, but that area *includes a town* (a seaside resort) that owes its prosperity to its good access – usually its beaches – to the sea. The ending "-side" is also found with other words meaning water, such as "riverside" and "lakeside", normally to stress the attractions of these places:

> *My parents moved to the seaside when my father retired.*
>
> *Bournemouth is a famous seaside resort on England's south coast, where many language schools operate.*

Strand

This is a flat accumulation of sand or gravel *formed by the action of the adjoining water*, especially when this is a river:

> *The street called The Strand in London was originally a quick and safe route across a deposit of sand formed in a bend of the Thames.*

Coast

This is *any strip of land that borders the sea*, but it is wide enough to include part of the nearby countryside:

> *New York is on the Atlantic coast of the USA.*

The preposition of position is "on" for all these words except **seaside**, in which case we say "at", probably because we think of the town as a point of reference.

16 BEGIN ~ START

1. We can say that, in general, these two verbs, which are used for activities and for movement, are completely synonymous:

    The match began / started on time but ended much later than anyone had expected.

    Here in the convent we begin / start every day with prayers.

    There's a lot to do, so let's begin / start now, shall we?

2. But we use **start** (not **begin**) in these cases:

    a) when it means *departure*:

    They started rather late and got caught in the rush hour.

    b) when it refers to the *functioning of some kind of machine*:

    How on earth did you manage to start that stupid engine?

    c) when a *signal* is given:

    A special pistol is fired to start the race.

    d) when it means *a sudden uncontrollable movement*:

    Goodness! How you made me start, creeping in silently like that!

    e) when we want to stress an *unexpected reaction*:

    He took one look at her and started laughing uproariously.

3. In talking about things that happen in a *natural or predictable way*, then **begin** is better:

    They say that life begins at forty, you know!

    Spring begins early in this part of the world.

17 BEGIN (TO) ~ START (TO)
(with infinitive or gerund)

When **begin** and **start** are followed by a second verb, it may appear either in the infinitive or in the gerundive form, and this difference changes the meaning of the sentence.

1. When the second verb is an infinitive, it means an *action that is interrupted or for some reason is not finished*:

   Mary started to speak, but then thought better of it and held her tongue.

   It had begun to rain as we left home, but in a little while the sun came out again and the clouds dissipated entirely.

2. When the second verb is a gerund, *we can assume that the action continues*:

   Now it began raining really hard, and we had to start looking for shelter.

   There wasn't much time before we were due to leave, so we started packing immediately after breakfast.

3. If the second verb is *stative* (that is, it is not possible to control the action it describes), *only an infinitive* is used:

   I suddenly began to feel very ill indeed and asked them to phone for a doctor.

   It was then that she started to see how she had gone wrong.

   You can't even begin to understand how I feel about it!

   By five o'clock, it was starting to get dark.

   They were beginning to receive unfavourable comments from the public about his behaviour off duty.

4. However, if there is no following verb at all, then we are talking either about *departure* or about making some kind of *machine function*, and in this case only **start** is possible:

   They started rather late and got caught in the rush hour.

   How on earth does one start this stupid engine?

5. Finally, a recommendation: if **begin** or **start** is itself used in the –ing form (the gerund, one of the continuous (progressive) tenses, or as a Present Participle), *for the sake of euphony* put the second verb into the *infinitive* form:

> *Beginning to accept your responsibilities is a sure sign of growing up.*
> (Not: "beginning accepting ...").

> *We're beginning to make real progress in this field now.*

> *When starting to lift the stone I cut my hand rather badly.*

18 BETWEEN ~ AMONG

Between

This word contains the linguistic element *tw-*, which almost always means *duality*, so if this preposition is used, it refers to only *two things* at a time.

1. For position, we say something is (or is not) **between** two others; and for lengths of time, we can use **between** instead of "from ... till ..." when the period is less precise:

> *The spot between the two trees was bare of grass.*

> *Between you and me, I think she's having an affair with him.*

> *Nothing stood between him and certain death if he moved.*

> *Shop hours are from nine till six, but you can find me there between about eight-thirty and six-thirty.*

2. Even if you see three or more referred to, no matter how large the number, the writer is considering *only two of them* each time:

> *Bacteria can get into the spaces between your teeth.*
> Of course, you have more than two teeth!

3. We also use **between** for movement – in this case from one point to another and back:

> *The ferry goes between Dover and Calais.*

4. Again, for movement we can say that something passes **between** *several objects*, because at one moment it is **between** two of them and the next moment **between** two different ones:

> *The road wound between the hills.*

5. **Between** is regularly used with "difference" or similar words when several objects are being considered:

> *The differences between all these varieties of pine are of more interest to botanists than to the general public.*

By the way, we never say "between both ...", perhaps because the word "both" means *two together*; instead you should say, "between them" or "between (the / these / his, etc.) two ...".

Among

In contrast, **among** refers to *more than two*, and often to quite a large number.

1. For position, it has the sense of *being mixed*:

> *I found a couple of silver coins among the copper ones.*
>
> *She lived among the Tuaregs for some months.*

2. For movement (in a large number), the sense is of *thorough penetration* – and not just to reach the other side but with a special purpose:

> *Day after day the good lady went among the common people, handing out alms to the needy.*
>
> *Plainclothes detectives walk about among the crowds in the store.*

19 BIG ~ LARGE ~ GREAT ~ GREATER ~ GRAND

Although all of these refer, directly or indirectly, to size, the differences are worth noting.

Big

A totally subjective adjective, in which what counts is the *importance* in the speaker's view rather than actual size; its opposite is "little":

> *The big toe is not only the largest of the five but is the one that propels us forward when we walk.*

> *Besides being older than you, your big brother is likely to be someone you admire and look for protection to.*

> *A big man may indeed be physically tall and corpulent, but he also radiates assurance and self-confidence.*

> *The big city is a place that offers what our hometown cannot: anonymity, fun, promise of success ... – in short, whatever we most want.*

Large

This, in contrast, is objective. That is, most people would agree on *the pure size aspect*: the object in question has a lot of mass. Its opposite is "small":

> *I'm afraid this television set would be too large for my living-room.*

> *The larger the city, the more dangerous life there is likely to be.*

Great

Another subjective word, used to describe abstract nouns, especially *qualities we admire* in someone or something:

> *The poor old dog approached us with great caution, its tail between its legs.*

> *A great man is one who has achieved fame or renown and is remembered for his contribution to the world.*

It also forms part of the name of a group of nations united politically, as in "Great Britain".

We must not confuse this use with the popular meaning of strong approval, as in the exclamation "Great!" when we like a suggestion very much.

Greater

We find this adjective used with the name of a city to denote its complete metropolitan area, including all its suburbs, as in Greater London.

Grand

This has no connotation of size but is a rather colloquial alternative for "majestic", "imposing", "awesome", etc.:

> *Society weddings are often very grand affairs, with everyone dressed in the height of fashion.*

However, it is often used as part of a name to describe the principal parts of buildings, gardens, and so on, as in the "Grand Staircase" of a palace.

Geographically, when a group of islands is known collectively by the name of the largest of these, this island is called "Grand ...", as in Grand Canary.

20 BORDER ~ FRONTIER ~ BOUNDARY

Owing to the transatlantic confusion of these terms, a full explanation is very desirable.

Border

Originally the word meant simply the line that separates the territories of two politically independent states. Nowadays we find it used, in Europe, wherever two adjoining states are so closely associated that *no passport is required* in crossing this line, as between England and Scotland or between other physically contiguous countries within the European Union.

In North America, the word **border** was used in this way between the early colonial states, especially when they belonged to the same European nation, and there **border** has remained the word for the divisions not only between the states of the USA but also between these and Canada or Mexico. For this reason citizens of the United States still tend to use this term for the line between any other two nations, because **frontier** has a special meaning to an American. **Borders** are usually announced at the roadside (often with a "Welcome" notice) but have no further importance to members of the public.

Frontier

During the nineteenth century, political tensions between many countries in Europe grew to the point where their borders became barriers, patrolled by policemen and customs officers, and special entry permits were demanded. Travellers from Britain soon came to use the French term "frontière" to describe this phenomenon, and consequently **frontier** (to a Briton) implies passports, visas, customs investigations, and other tiresome formalities.

In North America the territorial separation between the English and French colonies was a wild no-man's land, fiercely disputed and constantly changing, and the English colonials naturally adopted the French word, in its anglicized form, for this distinctive zone. Even after France had lost all its colonies there, the word **frontier** kept its meaning as "the uncivilized, and unclaimed, wilderness to the west", which is largely why this term is more metaphorical than literal to the modern American – and to all English-speakers, come to that.

Boundary

This term has always been used for lesser territorial and (especially) for local administrative divisions –those between counties or boroughs, for instance. A **boundary** is hardly ever indicated and its existence and its precise course are known (and are important) only to the authorities who determined it.

21 BOTH ~ THE TWO

Although these refer to two things – and not more than two – in each case, there is an important difference in use as well as in meaning.

Both

A very emphatic adjective (or pronoun), this is the indicator of *duality* and *reciprocity*, so it includes:

- any objects that occur *naturally in pairs* (hands, feet, eyes, ears, arms, legs, eyebrows, etc.);

- two people who have the kind of *reciprocal relationship* to each other that will never change (father and mother, parent and child, twins, ancestor and descendant, predecessor and successor, etc.);

- two people whose *reciprocal relationship* depends on current circumstances (husband and wife, friends, lovers, rivals, enemies, employer and employee, buyer and seller, donor and recipient, etc.);

- the two *equal parts* of something else (the sides of a street, the banks of a river, the arms of a chair, etc.), when there cannot be more than two;

- two naturally *contrasting aspects* (male and female, good and bad, right and left, front and back, top and bottom, etc.)

When we use **both** with these, we are thinking of those two together and *emphasising what they have in common*. The main point to bear in mind is that **both** means *to an equal degree* or *as much in one case as in the other*:

> *She had developed cataract in both eyes.*
>
> *Both father and son are brilliant pianists.*
>
> *The wings in this species are grey in both sexes.*
>
> *Both Japan and Russia have an interest in these islands.*
>
> *After using both hands for years, he found it difficult to shave with only one.*

N.B. As **both** stresses duality by itself, we cannot use it with prepositional phrases that also stress this, such as "either of" or "between", so "She held it between both hands" is incorrect: we have to say "in ..." or "with ...".

The two

This refers to two things (or people, or organisations, etc.) that have nothing permanently in common and are not normally thought of as a group, but *in this exceptional case are being considered together*:

> *The frontier between Peru and Ecuador is still in dispute, and the presidents of the two countries are to meet next week to discuss the problem again.*
>
> To use **both** would mean that each of these men was co-president of Peru and Ecuador together!

N.B. Only **the two**, not **both**, can be used with verbs that imply a change in relationship – verbs such as "join" or "unite" – or that must by their nature refer to two things equally, such as "share" or "separate":

> *That evening Henry joined the two brothers for dinner.*

> *The demolition of the Berlin wall reunited the two halves of Germany more palpably than any document could.*

> *China and Russia propose to hold a conference on the frontier that the two share / that divides the two.*

N.B. **The two** is not used with items listed under **Both**.

22 BURNING

Apart from the usual **to burn**, there are many other verbs and these indicate distinctive forms of combustion. Here are the commonest:

BRAND ~ CAUTERIZE ~ CHAR ~ CREMATE ~ INCINERATE ~ IGNITE ~ SCALD ~ SCORCH ~ SEAR ~ SET ALIGHT ~ SET LIGHT TO ~ SET FIRE TO ~ SINGE ~ SMOULDER

Brand

To press a red-hot iron against the skin to burn it deeply enough for a permanent scar to remain:

> *Each steer is branded when young, in order to ensure that it can never be confused with those of other owners.*

Cauterize

A medical process that consists of burning a wound in the skin in order to prevent infection. The noun is cauterization:

> *As soon as the amputation had been carried out, the cut was cauterized while the patient was still under the anaesthetic.*

Char

To part-burn wood very slowly until it is completely blackened but still intact. This wood, called charcoal, can then be used for long-term combustion. Wood is often charred by accident, however:

> *After the fire, all that was left was the charred remains of wooden beams.*

Cremate

To burn a dead body, reducing it to ashes. The noun is **cremation**:

> *Both her parents had been interred, but she always said she wanted to be cremated.*

Incinerate

To burn unwanted material until nothing is left but ash. The noun is **incineration**:

> *This municipality is justly proud of its ultra-modern rubbish incineration plant.*

Ignite

To start a burning process. The noun is **ignition**:

> *You press the starter and a spark from the plug ignites the petrol, which starts the engine.*

Scald

To burn with steam or some very hot liquid, which may be intentional but is all-too often an accident:

> *The child had been seriously scalded when he pulled at the handle of a pot of boiling water.*

Scorch

To burn only the surface of something:

> *There was a brown mark where the cloth had been scorched at some time during the ironing.*

Sear

To burn deeply. This is used more metaphorically than literally:

> *The anguish they had suffered had been seared into their memory.*

Set alight, Set light to, Set fire to

To start burning something, whether by design or not:

> *A still-glowing cigarette-end thrown from a passing car had set fire to the grass bank beside the road.*

Singe

To burn the hair or feathers on an area of skin:

> *I singed my arm on the edge of the oven yesterday.*

Smoulder (US smolder)

To burn extremely slowly without flames and in some cases without smoke:

> *A short-circuit set light to the accumulated fluff under the escalator, which smouldered for hours out of sight before bursting into flames.*

23 BY ~ IN ~ ON
(when used with a gerund)

These three prepositions often precede the gerund of a verb in order to explain a meaningful consequence, but each one has its distinctive effect on that consequence.

By

This serves to tell us the *intended result* of the action mentioned:

> *By leading his army across the Rubicon and thus provoking a civil war, Julius Caesar saved himself from certain impeachment, political disgrace, and probable death.*

In

This tells us the *unintended result* of the action:

> *In leading his army across the Rubicon and thus provoking a civil war, Julius Caesar brought about a complete change in Rome's system of government.*

On

This time the preposition, instead of indicating the result, *means "when"* and always refers to a specific moment in the past or future:

> *On leading his army across the Rubicon, Caesar's first act was to ensure the support of the nearest towns.*

24 CHANGE ~ ALTER ~ SWITCH ~ EXCHANGE ~ INTERCHANGE

Alter and **Change** (in that order)

1. We use **alter** to refer especially to the *appearance*, rather than the substance of something. If we **alter** anything, we do something to its aspect that makes it look different, and in its intransitive form the verb has the same external sense: the countryside **alters** from season to season, but it remains the same area of land. Similarly, people **alter** outwardly: after a time, their faces, bodies, and hair-colour no longer look the same as before; but if they **change** it happens inwardly: it is the character that is becoming different, and this may or may not manifest itself on the surface.

2. We frequently use **change** for quite simple actions:

> *Could you change this twenty-pound note for me?*
> The note will be replaced by several of smaller value.

Compare the difference in these sentences:

   a) *Do we have to change for dinner in this hotel?*
       Do we have to put special clothes on?

   b) *I'm going to change this dress.*
       ...take this one off and put on a different dress *or* ...take this dress back to the shop and ask for a different model.

   c) *I'm going to alter this dress.*
       Make its shape different.

3. **Change** often implies speed and a clear difference from one state to the next, whereas **alter** seems to require time and *the difference is subtler to detect*:

    > *When I told him my opinion of his plan, his face changed.*
    > He showed an instant reaction to my words.

    > *His new dentures had altered his face in some way.*

4. Another difference is that **change** can mean *movement* from one place to another:

    > *The artist changed his brush to the other hand in order to steady the easel.*

    > *We had to change trains at Birmingham.*
    > We had to enter a different train.

    > *All change, please!*
    > Everybody must leave this train.

Switch

This word works, like a computer, on the binary principle: there are only two possible states – from one to the other - and *the movement is immediate*, just like a light-switch: on or off. And transitively, if we **switch** (two) objects we move each *quickly* to the position of the other:

> *Halfway through the lecture the speaker switched abruptly to a totally different theme, leaving the audience at a loss to follow him.*

> *The two suspects switched briefcases so adroitly that the watching police utterly failed to detect the movement and so were unable to make an arrest.*

Exchange and Interchange

Exchange requires *two objects* and we **exchange** one *for* (note the preposition) the other. The reason is that now one has more importance for us than the other; this is why we use **exchange** (the noun) for conversion of currencies:

> *Before commencing negotiations, tribal chiefs always exchange gifts, the visitor's customarily being of greater value than that or those of his host.*

But **interchange** needs *several objects* (and the action of several parties) at the same time:

The president of the school's "old boys" association had difficulty in being heard in the hubbub because its members were far too busy interchanging greetings and news, all at the same time.

N.B. To get a clearer idea of the difference between these, see **Between.**

25 CHARACTER ~ PERSONALITY

Character

When well distinguished, **character** describes the internal *compound of mental and emotional qualities that define an individual*. The essence of our character is born with us and develops as we do. Being so fundamental, it is not easily seen and analysed, and may in fact be a mystery to the individual himself. However, it tends to remain constant, and if it changes this is in most cases the result of some traumatic experience:

They say that suffering is the greatest test of character; it brings out the best and the worst in us.

There are certain facets of his character that only very occasionally appear and leave one intrigued as to what kind of man he really is.

Personality

On the other hand, **personality** is the external *manifestation of a character* – what we reveal to the world: the way we behave in front of others (or even when alone, to please ourselves). It is evident in details like tone of voice, style of dressing, choice of home, and so on, which are all very clear to other people and leave some kind of impression. Extroverts, for instance, are people whose personality is exceptionally strong and makes an immediate impact:

He was a man of forceful personality, the kind of person one could never forget.

The actress's loud voice and flamboyant way of dressing are simply part of her extravagant personality.

It is only when we use these words to describe enduring things like places (buildings, towns, countries, ...) that the difference between them is likely to disappear.

26 CITY ~ TOWN ~ VILLAGE ~ HAMLET ~ BOROUGH

Hamlet

Let's begin with the smallest of these: a **hamlet** is nothing more than a group of a few homes inhabited by different families. There is no communal centre, not even a church, and the access to it is usually not a through-road.

Village

A **village** is large enough to have a few streets, a number of shops, and one (or more) churches. It has a central area too: a small square in Continental villages and an open area of grass called "the green" in English ones; but as a village in Britain has no officially recognised administration there is no public building for it.

Town

In the USA a **town** stands halfway in size between **village** and **city**, but in Britain it is anything larger than a village, *no matter how big it is*. Its essential characteristics are: streets with pavements and buildings on both sides, street lighting at night, a clearly central area, its own local police force and a centrally situated administrative building called the "town hall".

Towns which hold periodic markets, to which the local country people bring their wares, are called **market towns**. (Also see **Town, Country, Countryside, Landscape**).

City

This is a word of Latin origin and in Europe retains most of its Roman connotations. A European town is termed **city** when a) it is the capital of the nation; b) it is an important administrative centre; c) it was of Roman founding; or d) it is the seat of a bishop, in which case its main church is a cathedral. For this reason London contains two **cities**: the City of London and the City of Westminster.

In the USA the term **city** is used to distinguish the town from the state of the same name, as in the case of New York City / State, but many quite small towns are called "City" even though they have no special importance and do not seem to deserve this title in any way.

Borough

A **borough** in Britain is technically a town represented by a Member of Parliament, but in practical terms it is an administrative division of a large town, usually with its own "town hall". In the USA, a **borough** is any town recognised as a municipality in its own right, and, as in Britain, frequently forms part of a larger community.

27 CLASSIC ~ CLASSICAL

Classical

Let's begin with **classical**. We use this to describe *a style* in certain of the arts – notably the architecture that exploits features developed by the ancient Greeks and Romans, and the music of the later eighteenth century:

> *The column, fluted or otherwise, is a characteristic of classical building techniques.*

> *Classical composers such as Haydn had to make do with the less well developed instruments of their period.*

Classic (noun and adjective)

It is used of one case that is outstandingly *representative of a whole "class"* or group of things:

> *This anthology covers the full range of nineteenth-century Russian classics* (= the most famous books), *with special emphasis on Tolstoy.*

> *We found ourselves in the classic* (= typical) *situation of possessing plenty of money, but not in a form that we could use: our costly traveller's cheques were refused everywhere.*

28 CONSIST OF ~ CONSIST IN

A simple explanation is that **consist** with **of** refers to more than one component, while with **in** there is only one, but that explanation needs further explaining!

Consist of

When we talk about *the various parts* that make up a whole, we use **consist of**:

> *A three-piece suite consists of a settee (or sofa) plus two armchairs, all in the same style and upholstered in the same material.*

> *The estate you are interested in buying consists of the house itself, with its double garage, the two gardens, and sundry outhouses, a row of three eighteenth-century cottages (all at present unoccupied), and forty acres of arable land.*

Consist in

We use **consist in** when we want to explain that an abstract concept can be *represented by an action or course of behaviour*:

> *Blind faith consists in believing something without wanting, or needing, proof of its truth.*

> *When I was told that the job would consist in holding the door open whenever someone wanted to enter or leave the hotel and calling taxis for guests who asked for one, and it would be paid accordingly, I turned it down flat.*

29 CONTAMINATE ~ POLLUTE

In modern use, due mainly to changes in industrial processes, an important distinction has developed between these two verbs.

Contaminate

Basically, this means *transfer dirt or infection from a soiled object to something that was previously clean*. The contamination is usually organic:

Always wash your hands well before touching food to avoid contaminating it.

Unprotected meat or fish can easily be contaminated with bacteria from flies, which have acquired them by feeding on rotting food.

In her family's opinion, her association with the rebels had "contaminated" her political views.

Pollute

Here the meaning, which is now ecological, is *soil an area of the environment*. The areas referred to include the atmosphere, the sea, rivers, lakes, etc. and the pollution is mostly chemical:

Acid rain has polluted many Scandinavian lakes, killing off all forms of life in them.

A massive oil spill last winter polluted a whole stretch of the coast, rendering these beaches unusable for the coming tourist season.

30 CONTROL ~ CHECK ~ TEST ~ PROVE ~ TRY ~ TRY OUT

Control

This is the most difficult of these verbs to understand, because its modern use differs in English from the use in other languages. In most cases it means *limiting or directing the movement and flow of something*. In other words, something that would naturally move in a certain direction or at a certain speed is obliged to change direction or reduce its flow. What kind of thing are we contemplating here? Well, things that move and whose movements are regarded as potentially dangerous in some way, such as the current of a river, the movement of traffic, variations of temperature, the behaviour of an animal, or one's temper. If any of these is allowed to move freely, the result could be very harmful: the river might overflow, the volume or speed of the traffic could lead to accidents, a sudden rise in temperature might damage something, etc.:

When driving a car we can use either the brake or the gears to control the speed.

Please control your tongue, Bill. If you say the first thing that comes into your head every time, you can easily annoy somebody else.

The blending rate of the components in this experiment has to be systematically controlled at all times, otherwise we have no guarantee that the results will be valid.

N.B. There is one classic situation in which **control** is used in the "Continental" sense: "Passport Control". In the modern sense in English, passports cannot really be controlled, because they are completely inert objects which don't do anything and therefore cannot cause trouble: but the use of this phrase is justified because it is so easily recognised by travellers.

Check

This means *looking at something (once or repeatedly) to be sure that there has been or is no change*. We do this with things like the time (and for this we look at watches and clocks), information already given, or a list of things to do:

I'm not sure of his telephone number, so I'd better check it in the directory.

Did you remember to check what time the plane leaves?

This little machine checks that each envelope bears a correct stamp.

Test

When we **test** something, we use it experimentally, to see *whether its behaviour is what is wanted:*

On completion, every one of these machines is tested rigorously so that any defects may be corrected before it leaves the factory.

Prove

What we **prove** is facts or the truth of a belief or theory, and we do this by *convincing other people* (by presenting irrefutable evidence):

His fingerprints in the room proved that he had been there at some time.

Galileo knew that the Earth was round, but he did not have the means to prove it to his contemporaries.

I know you have this marvellous theory about the emotions, but how can you prove that it's true?

Try (Also see **Unexpected applications**)

When you **try** something (not try *to do* something), you *use it experimentally* – to see *whether* it works, not *how* it works. And in the case of food and drink, you put a little in your mouth – only a little, in case you don't like it! This requires actions like pushing, tasting, feeling – anything, in fact, that is *done tentatively* because we don't know what will happen as a result:

> *She tried the doorbell, but it was evidently out of order.*

> *After trying English, French, and Italian, all in vain, on these people, I had no further language possibilities and had to sit in silence for the rest of the journey.*

> *I offered him a sip of the drink I had been given and was most amused to see how apprehensively he tried it.*

Try out

This time you *make the object work* because you don't know yet how well it will do it. Or if it is something you have learnt to do, you practise it for perhaps the first time, watching to see *how successfully* you do it:

> *This is an excellent track for trying out new cars.*

> *Good, now we've made the machine, so the next thing is to try it out in a real situation and see how it performs.*

> *The young wife tried her cooking out on her brother before she dared present it to her husband.*

31 CONVINCE ~ PERSUADE ~ DISSUADE

Although these verbs look similar, there are differences of meaning and of use that are well worth studying.

Convince

The basic meaning of this verb is *to make someone believe a fact*, which is usually done by presenting proof. We convince a person *that something is true* or we convince him *of a fact*; **convince** is *not* followed by an infinitive:

> *It was circumnavigation of the globe that finally convinced the sceptics that the world was not flat.*

Her husband convinced her of the need to find a babysitter by showing her how tired it left him to look after the children on his own.

Persuade

This verb means *to use arguments to make someone do something*. Observe that the purpose is not to make him believe anything but to induce him to do it (usually by talking), even though he may not be convinced of its necessity. We can persuade him *that something is a fact* or (especially) *to do something*.

If the other person intends to do something that we don't think is wise, we **persuade** him *not* to do it:

Nigel persuaded his family that he ought to find a job instead of going to university.

It was my children who finally persuaded me to move to a better district, and now I'm glad I listened to them.

The union delegate persuaded the workers not to accept their management's pay offer.

Dissuade

This verb has the same effect as *to persuade not to ...* but it is followed by *from ... (+ a gerund)*. In many cases it has the same meaning as *deter*.

The driver dissuaded me from smoking in his taxi.

The crowd was dissuaded from attacking the football referee only by the presence of armed police.

It was only the presence of armed police that dissuaded the crowd from attacking the football referee.

32 CUTTING
(Ways of Cutting)

**CARVE ~ CHOP ~ CLEAVE ~ GASH ~ GOUGE ~ HACK ~
INCISE ~ LOP ~ NICK ~ PARE ~ PEEL ~ PRUNE ~ SAW ~
SCORE ~ SCRATCH ~ SEVER ~ SHAVE ~
SHEAR ~ SLASH ~ SLICE ~ SLIT ~
SNIP ~ TRIM ~ WHITTLE**

Carve

This is the artistic method of cutting. You use some kind of knife to cut away unwanted parts of the basic material (usually wood), and *what is left is the shape you desire.* At table, this is the verb for cutting a large piece of meat into individual portions:

The oak panel at the bed-head had been carved to represent scenes from the Old Testament.

Father's way of carving the Christmas turkey used to please everyone because he made sure we all got a part of the meat we most liked.

Chop

To cut something into smaller parts. The firm texture of the material requires a heavy, sharp-edged instrument (a chopper, axe, or cleaver) that is applied with *forceful movements*, generally downwards and onto a hard surface:

The sawn logs had next to be chopped into smaller pieces that would fit into the average fireplace.

Cleave

To cut something into two more or less equal parts *in one blow* (or only a few blows) with a very heavy instrument:

The old battle-axe wielded by the Vikings was capable of cleaving a man's head down to the neck.

Gash

To cut *long and deeply* in one violent movement:

> *She gashed her arm badly on a jagged piece of glass from the broken window and was rushed to hospital before she could lose too much blood.*

Gouge

To cut deeply in order to *leave a deep hole* or to extract something in one movement:

> *You can use the curved point on this knife to gouge out any "eyes" in the potato you're peeling.*

Hack

To cut repeatedly with *quick, heavy, but inexpert blows*. If used with "at", it shows that the cutting is ineffectual:

> *They managed to hack through the dense jungle vegetation with the axe in their equipment, although a proper Indian machete would have done it much more efficiently.*

Incise

To cut into an object *with care and precision*, especially as a surgeon does it when operating:

> *The boar's tusk had been beautifully incised with tiny figures representing pagan gods or heroes in battle.*

Lop

To cut off *smaller parts from something large*, like a tree, in single blows:

> *The best thing is to lop the branches off first; then you can see clearly how to fell the tree itself.*

Nick

To make a *very small cut*, perhaps by accident:

> *Jim had nicked himself while shaving and there was a tiny scab of dried blood on his chin.*

Pare

To cut away *the skin of a fruit* or *the rind of a* cheese. This usually needs care and good eyesight:

> *At one time people used the same small knife for paring apples and their fingernails.*

Peel

Like **pare**, to *cut or pull off* the skin of a fruit or vegetable or the bark of a tree:

> *She's in the kitchen, peeling potatoes for lunch.*

Prune

To cut off *chosen parts of a plant* so as to make it grow more strongly:

> *Only a gardener knows when and how to prune the bushes to get the best flowers the following year.*

Saw

To cut *with a saw*, using a regular forward-backward movement:

> *My cousin had managed to saw halfway through the tree trunk before he got too tired to finish the job.*

Score

To make a number of (shallow and usually parallel) *cuts across the surface* of something. There are various reasons for this: to record debts or points gained in sports, or the passage of time (as in prison), or when preparing a roast, or simply to record your presence (as at school):

> *Before putting the leg of pork in the oven, she scored the skin several times and then salted it.*
>
> *The waiting-room wall was badly scored where impatient people had pushed their chairs against it.*

Scratch

To make the *lightest of cuts* on a surface, using a fingernail or some pointed object:

> *In parts of Africa the soil is so hard that ploughing is more a matter of scratching the surface than of real agriculture.*

Sever

Not a common verb nowadays, but it means *dividing or cutting off a part* from the rest, normally with a single blow:

> *The tribal punishment for theft included the grim possibility of having a hand severed.*

Shave

We all know this as cutting hair off the body, but it also means cutting *very thin layers* from other kinds of surface:

> *The carpenter shaved off the old veneer from the table, revealing the beautiful grain of walnut wood beneath.*

Shear

To cut *right through an object in one movement*, or to *cut off the wool* on a sheep:

> *A large piece of corrugated iron, wrenched from the roof by the gale, whirled down, shearing two fingers off his hand.*
>
> *The ewes, recently shorn of their wool, now looked scrawny and undernourished.*

Slash

To make a *sudden long cut* across or down something:

> *Unable to find any division in the curtain, he drew his sword and slashed it open in one sweep.*

Slice

To cut into *several equally thick (or thin) sections*:

> *We always buy sliced bread, you know, because it comes ready for toasting that way.*

Slit

To open or divide something by making one *straight cut along* or down it:

> *There was a narrow-bladed knife in the drawer and I used that to slit the envelope open.*

Snip

To use scissors to make *quick, small cuts*:

> *One by one she snipped through the tiny stitches that held the material together.*

Trim

To cut off all uneven ends, leaving *a regular surface*. We do this to our own hair, to the fur of a dog, and to trees and bushes to which we want to give a distinctive shape:

> *I must get the barber to trim my beard again soon.*

Whittle

To cut away to reduce thickness or to cut the end of something in such a way as *to obtain a point*:

> *He whittled the end of the stick until it was sharp enough to serve as a spear.*

33 DAY
(prepositional phrases with units of time)

The time unit given in all the following cases happens to be the word "day", but any other recognized unit of time can be used, such as: moment, minute, hour, week, month, year, etc., as shown in the examples.

Day by day

We use this phrase to show steady *progress* and development:

> *Once she had passed the first stage of convalescence her improvement was increasingly obvious, day by day.*
>
> *Week by week the tree grew taller and its foliage thicker.*

Day after day / Day in, day out

These two phrases stress the *repetition* or – especially – the *monotony* of the situation:

Morning after morning he went to open his mailbox, but there was never anything for him.

We could sit here night after night, waiting for the ghost to appear again, and do you think it ever will?

The life of a galley slave was to pull on the oar day in, day out, with only the hours of darkness for rest, constant beatings, and little or no guarantee of eventual release.

From day to day

Here the phrase means constant *changes* of situation (compare "from time to time" or "from place to place"):

All that week the weather varied so much from day to day that it began to look as if the expedition would never get under way before winter set in.

34 DESPAIR ~ DESPERATION

Despair

This means the *loss of all hope* (just as **to despair** consequently means *to lose all hope*). The person affected, seeing no solution to his problem, is prepared to take whatever drastic action will put an end to his anguish, and that often leads directly to suicide:

When it became clear, after so many months of unremitting siege by the Romans, that help was now impossible, in their despair the inhabitants of Numancia resolved to destroy their city and kill themselves rather than submit to certain enslavement.

Desperation

It is the state of mind of someone who sees his problem very clearly and realizes that the worst will happen *unless he does something at once*, so he acts without delay. What he does is often extremely dangerous and probably has very little chance of success, but he cannot simply wait for calamity to overtake him:

The fire had now cut him off altogether from access to the doors, so in desperation, he seized the axe and began hacking at the floor boards. There was a remote chance that he might cut a large enough hole before the flames reached him.

35 DIE ~ BE KILLED

Die

As dying is the end of living, we use **to die** in these cases:

- when a life comes to its *natural end*:

  Queen Anne had thirteen children, but they all died before she did.

  He died in his sleep at the ripe old age of 93.

  Do you think a wicked woman like that will go to heaven when she dies?

- when we specify the *terminal illness*:

  The fact that both her parents had died of cancer was taken into account when she applied for life assurance.

  She is supposed to have died of a broken heart.

  I think I'd die of boredom if I had to work there!

- when any living thing *suffers so much* (for whatever reason) that death is inevitable:

  The roses had not been watered for weeks and had all died.

  His second wife died in giving birth to his only son.

  He was still living when they got him out from the blazing house, but he died of his burns on the way to hospital.

Be killed

This indicates a *sudden, violent (and therefore unnatural) death*, whether accidental or procured:

He was killed when his plane crashed last year.

All the trees on the volcano's western slope were killed by a massive flood of lava from the eruption.

He was flung out of the car on a sharp bend and the car then overturned, killing him outright.

According to myth, Icarus was killed when he flew too close to the sun and his wax wings melted, precipitating him into the sea that still bears his name today.

Tradition says that he came to the throne by killing all his brothers in various ways.

However, when the death is *unusual or is caused by deliberate human action*, as in the last example, we prefer to use a more precise verb or verbal phrase that describes the manner of death:

> *My cousin was electrocuted while repairing a faulty plug.*
>
> *The Borgias are notorious for poisoning their enemies.*
>
> *He was reputedly torn to pieces by his own dogs.*
>
> *The last Tsar and his family were shot by a Soviet execution squad.*
>
> *Anne Boleyn was beheaded in the Tower of London.*
>
> *They say this is the spot where highwaymen and footpads used to be hanged.*

Consequently, it is more usual to say "He was killed in a car crash" (where the crash was the immediate cause of his death) than "He died in a car crash", which implies that his death was purely coincidental with the crash – that he suffered a heart attack or something similar that had nothing to do with the crash.

(Also see **Assassin, Assassination, Murder, Murderer, Killer**)

36 DIFFER ~ VARY

Differ

When people **differ**, they disagree because they have different, and probably contrary, opinions:

> *Husband and wife differed violently over the child's upbringing.*

Differ is not a transitive verb; to show that we recognise or find a difference between things, we have to use **distinguish** or **differentiate**:

> *I could never distinguish one twin from the other, unless I saw them together.*
>
> *You have to differentiate clearly between testing and trying out when referring to chemical products.*

Differ from

When two things are not the same in a certain respect (they are different), one **differs from** the other:

Men differ from women – physically and to some extent mentally.

Welsh differs enormously from English.

The countryside of Portugal differs completely from that of central Spain.

Vary

But when *one thing* is not constant at all times or in all the places where it exists, we say it **varies**:

The weather varies from day to day.
The weather is a single thing, but it undergoes many changes.

The climate varies from one part of the country to another.
The country is considered to have one climate, but this is **variable**, presenting different aspects in different districts.

As a transitive verb, we can **vary** what we are doing: although basically it is the same action, we make small changes in detail to provide **variety**:

He varied his routine by taking a slightly different route to work each day.

She was a totally predictable woman, who never varied her habits.

37 DIRTY ~ GRUBBY ~ GRIMY ~ FILTHY ~ FOUL

Dirty

Although we all know this because it means "not clean", you can use any of the above if the conditions are right. They are given in order of intensity. However **dirty** can replace any of the others if it is qualified by an adverb like "very" or "terribly".

Grubby

This is used for *clothing or for the personal appearance, especially the hands and face*, and in that case tends to describe children rather than adults, where the dirt is not the result of "honest work". The implication is that considerable cleaning will be necessary:

I had to rub very hard to clean the grubby knee patches on his little trousers.

Grimy

Besides the above possibilities, we can include *parts of buildings*. The dirt is so deeply ingrained that really long, hard cleaning will be needed:

Years of smoke and soot had left the wall too grimy to be cleaned by mere washing.

Filthy

Very dirty indeed: a tremendous amount of cleaning would be needed!

This room is absolutely filthy, John! It'll take me all day to make it look reasonably habitable again!

Foul

The strongest of all, especially *where smells are concerned*:

The prison was unbelievably overcrowded and the latrines were absolutely foul.

There was a foul smell inside, for the cave had been occupied by wild animals.

38 DOOR ~ GATE ~ DOORWAY ~ GATEWAY

Door

The two essential characteristics of a door are: that it forms part of a wall, which encloses it on either side and also above, and that it *leads into a room* of some kind.

Gate

A gate also forms part of some sort of enclosure, such as a **wall, fence** or **railing**, but unlike a door it *leads into a bounded space open to the sky* –a yard, a garden, a park,... For this reason **gate**, not **door**, is used in airports; in the days of the original aerodromes that preceded modern airports there was no building to go through and all that separated the waiting passengers from their plane was a fence with a gate.

Doorway and Gateway

These both refer to the *gap created* by opening a door or gate. Gateway is frequently used metaphorically, to describe a means of reaching some beautiful place or of attaining one's goal:

> *A large guard stood in the doorway, barring our path.*
>
> *Welcome to Dover – gateway to the Continent.*

39 DUCK ~ COWER ~ CRINGE ~ GROVEL
(all verbs)

Duck

We **duck** (*lower the head quickly*) when we realise that we are likely to hit our head on something low:

> *Being such a tall man, he had to duck each time he entered.*

Cower

This verb shows a position of the body in which both the back and the shoulders are bent suddenly. It is an *instinctive movement, mostly prompted by fear*:

> *The child cowered against the wall in an attempt to avoid being hit as the man raised his fist.*

Cringe

This action is always caused by fear or terror: the knees too are bent, bringing the body *closer to the ground, away from impending danger*:

> *His dog cringed when he shouted, fearing another blow.*

Grovel

In this case the person (or animal, especially a dog) moves forward with the whole body lying on the ground, as flat as possible, indicating *utter abjection and humility*. It is very often used figuratively, of course:

> *The female generally approaches the male grovelling, in case he attacks her before realizing her intentions.*

> *He had no time for people who grovelled before their masters and made no effort to fight for their freedom.*

40 EARN ~ GAIN ~ WIN

English seems to have three verbs for what are only two in other languages, and this leads to confusion for foreigners.

Earn

This indicates receiving something of value (especially money) *in return for work or some similar constant effort*. What is received is, furthermore, – or should be – in direct proportion to the effort made for this purpose:

> *He earned enough in his new job to be able to put down a deposit for a house after only six months.*

Gain

In this case you obtain what you want or something that benefits you, but *the means is not indicated or even implied*, nor is there any suggestion of effort:

> *As a direct result of the war, each of the victors gained considerable territory.*

Win

What is obtained here is something of great value or is very much desired, but the success in obtaining it is regarded either as *a matter of luck* or as *a due reward for the – special – effort made*:

> *She won the first prize for sports at school.*

41 EARTH ~ LAND ~ GROUND ~ SOIL

As these words all refer to more or less the same place, the differences between them are essentially a matter of concept: that is, how we consider each one.

Earth

In addition to being the name of our planet (generally spelt with a capital E) and one of the four elements (earth, air, fire and water) of medieval times, **earth** is basically *a material*, something we use in construction works and building, and in this sense it represents *plain reality*:

> *Most African huts have floors made of beaten earth instead of wood or stone, as in Europe.*

> *You're living in a fantasy, Emma; come down to earth and see matters as they really are!*

Land

This is approximately the same as *territory*. That is, areas of this planet that we can own and buy or sell:

> *"This land is my land, this land is your land..."* (A well-known American song).

> *He owns all the best land in this country.*

> *"Land of hope and glory..."* (A patriotic English song).

As a verb, it means *arrival from the air or the sea*:

> *The plane is due to land in twenty minutes' time.*

> *When, after sailing round the world, he finally landed in New Zealand, he was greeted with acclamations as a hero.*

Ground

There are three meanings to this word:

1. The *surface of the earth* – something we can measure and mark out:

   He took a stick and drew lines on the ground to show where the streets of his new city would be laid out.

2. The *solidity* of the earth as opposed to the fluidity of the air, although this characteristic can be a problem for aircraft (to be grounded), and for sea craft (to go aground):

   It was a relief to feel himself on the ground again after the giddy movements of the balloon.

   Our little boat suddenly stopped moving: we had gone aground on a sandbank.

   "They've grounded me as a punishment", said the pilot sadly, "so I'm not allowed to fly for two weeks."

3. *Reality*, as with **earth**:

   Enid's a thoroughly practical girl; she's got her feet on the ground all right.

Soil

Again, there are two interpretations to this word:

1. The quality and value of the earth for agricultural and ecological purposes:

   They've enriched the soil with fertilizers and now it's producing better crops than ever.

   If any more of the soil is eroded by the wind and the heavy rain, we shall soon have pre-desert conditions.

2. As a verb, **to soil** means to make what was clean dirty:

   She would never soil her beautiful hands with housework!

   They're holding a sale of shop-soiled articles all next week.
   Articles that have become marked or have lost colour through being handled by customers or being exposed in the window.

42 ECONOMIC ~ ECONOMICAL

Economic

It is the adjective associated with the *economy* (of a country) or the *science of economics* (the study of the use of money):

> *A national bank serves mainly these days to regulate the economic state of the nation.*

Economical

It is the equivalent of *cheap*, in the sense of *saving expense* (or effort):

> *Hypermarkets work on the principle that it is more economical* (= cheaper) *for the customer to buy once in a large quantity than often in small amounts.*

43 END ~ ENDING ~ FINISH

End (noun)

The opposite of "beginning" and therefore the point or instant at which *a thing ceases to be*. The important consideration is that this point is reached naturally; nothing is done to force it:

> *You'll see a large red-brick church at the end of this road; that's where you should turn off.*

> *The suspense is maintained brilliantly, keeping the reader intrigued throughout the book, but the many threads come together and everything is made clear at the end.*

> *After a life of such success, it is ironic that the end should be so tragic.*

To end

In its intransitive form, this simply tells us *when or how the end of something comes* – no matter whether it is desired or not:

> *The party, which had begun so amicably, ended in bloodshed.*

But the transitive form indicates that someone *has a special reason for terminating* something or *terminates it before its natural time-limit*:

He ended the letter with a pathetic plea for forgiveness.

Distraught at such a loss, he resolved to end his life there and then.

The outbreak of the revolution ended their plans to reform the system.

Ending (noun only)

This term, which is used exclusively for *things that are told or described* (that is, all kinds of narrative), is the particular way the author or storyteller brings his story – poem, book, film, play, etc. – to an end:

Tragic operas always have such dramatic endings, don't they?

The children listened tensely as he recounted the fairy-tale, afraid that there was going to be an unhappy ending.

Finish (noun)

This was originally only a racing term, used for the post or other object that marked the point at which the contestants had *to stop* running, but now it is applied to situations that have nothing to do with sports, such as the *final touch* to something created:

A good artisan makes sure that the finish he gives to his work is in every way as fine as the workmanship and materials that were employed in its design and execution.

To finish

As with **to end**, the intransitive form tells us when or how an end comes, but with the implication that it is so designed *because the original purpose has been fulfilled*:

The meeting had finished before I could get there.

The transitive form similarly indicates completion – someone brings something to an end because *there is nothing more to be done*:

It took him three years to finish the symphony to his full satisfaction.

For materials and food or drink it means *"consume it all"*:

Can't anyone finish this last bit of pudding? It won't keep another day.

44 ENTRANCE ~ ENTRY

Entrance

This is the *opening* that gives access to a place, including all kinds of **doors** and **gates**. If you see a sign announcing "No entrance", it means that the object in front of you is not the entrance it seems to be, but is perhaps only a false door:

> *To avoid being caught by the paparazzi outside, famous people often leave the court by the rear entrance.*

> *The sentries on either side of the palace entrance are all-too used to being photographed by enthusiastic tourists.*

Entry

1. This is the *action of entering* a place. The common sign "No entry" means either that the public may not enter the building at this point (in other words, you must find another entrance) or that traffic may not enter the street from this end:

    > *He made his entry to the accompaniment of flutes and drums.*

    > *The march they are playing is called "The Entry of the Gladiators". It's when they come into the arena, I suppose.*

2. A second meaning is *something written* in an important record book, such as a ledger or register (or a computer):

    > *The registry office said they could find no marriage entry for the date we had given them, which was most alarming.*

    > *You can delete a wrong entry by simply pressing this key.*

    > *The first entry in "¿Y cuál es la diferencia? - So What's the Difference?" is the problem item "able", on page 9.*

45 FAMOUS ~ NOTORIOUS

Famous (noun: fame)

This tends to be *a favourable term*: we admire the person or his or her actions or approve of those. But careful: in personal relationships we often use this adjective ironically to describe someone's *bad habits*:

> *Chinese proverbs are famous for their wisdom.*
>
> *My brother is famous for forgetting his wife's birthday, year after year.*

Notorious (noun: notoriety)

This is nowadays a negative word. It certainly means fame, but for action or behaviour that we *disapprove of*, and in this sense it can be used, like **famous**, in personal relationships, but this time without the irony:

> *Madame Tussaud's "Chamber of Horrors" includes all of Britain's really notorious criminals.*
>
> *Nero is – perhaps unjustly – Rome's most notorious emperor.*
>
> *Simon's notorious for always getting drunk at parties, I'm sorry to say.*

46 FATAL ~ DEADLY ~ DEATHLY ~ LETHAL ~ MORTAL

Although all these adjectives are related to the idea of death, each one expresses something different.

Fatal

In its strictest sense, this means *causing death, but usually without intending it*, so a fatal accident is one in which someone is killed:

> *If your father has another stroke now, it will probably be fatal; you must be prepared for the worst.*

But used more loosely it is a synonym of *dire* or *disastrous*:

> *That small change in the weather turned out to be fatal to our picnic plans.*

Deadly

This describes something that is *designed for killing* or is *used with the intention of killing*, such as a large dose of poison:

> *A sling is a deadly weapon in the hands of an expert.*
>
> *He threw the spear with such deadly accuracy that it felled his opponent instantly.*

Deathly

Use this for *anything that looks or sounds or feels dead*, such as intense pallor of face, an utter silence, or very cold hands. There is also an adverb with exactly the same form, used mainly before adjectives of colour or temperature.

> *The deathly whiteness of her face showed how grave her illness was.*

Lethal

Used for normally harmless objects *used dangerously* or products that *in certain amounts cause death*:

> *Even a child's catapult can become lethal if used with the necessary skill and precision.*
>
> *Small amounts of this snake's venom are virtually harmless, but large doses are always lethal.*

Mortal

1. One meaning, for all living organisms, is *destined to die* (the opposite of immortal), and in this sense the word is also a noun, used only for human beings:

> *His heel, being the one part of Achilles that was mortal, was the only part of his body that could be wounded.*

2. The other meaning, for *injuries* of all kinds, is *serious enough to cause death* and it shares this meaning with **fatal**:

In most people a broken collar-bone has no serious consequences, but for a man of William's age it proved mortal/fatal.

The arrow that had penetrated his lung caused a mortal wound, from which he died ten days later.

47 FIND ~ MEET ~ ENCOUNTER ~ MEET WITH ~ RUN INTO ~ COME ACROSS ~ DISCOVER ~ LOCATE ~ DETECT

Find

1. This is the general verb, the one it is possible to use instead of any of the others, but at the same time the least precise of all. We use it mostly when *something that was lost reappears* or when *the existence of something becomes known*:

    Has anyone found the lighter I lost in this room last week?

    In the nineteenth century gold was found in Alaska.

2. Another important use is to show the *strange circumstances* of the thing or person at the moment of being found:

    The president was found lying dead across his desk.

3. Also when used for people, it means that the person was behaving in an *unexpected or totally uncharacteristic* way:

    She found her husband hopelessly drunk in the cellar.

Meet

We use this verb when describing contact with people only. The contact may be *arranged or accidental*, and it is the only verb possible when we refer to the *first contact of all between them*:

    Can you meet me sometime this week – somewhere convenient to both of us?

    You meet all kinds of people in this job, as you'll soon see.

My husband and I met at university, you know.

Encounter

This verb has a rather negative sense: the thing we find is certainly *not expected*, such as a new situation, and is often *something we didn't want to find*, like some kind of obstacle:

The advancing army encountered stiff resistance from the local militia.

N.B.   Used in a negative situation, **encounter** means *not finding the obstacle expected*:

They encountered no opposition when they introduced the new regulations.

Meet with

As with **encounter**, it shows the existence of an obstacle (one that is not physical) that *could have been expected*:

My plan to change our breakfast cereal met with disbelief and dismay among my children.

Run into

1.   Another indication of an obstacle, expected or not, but this time it is *likely to be physical*:

Halfway down the mountain, the climbers ran into dense fog and had to wait for it to clear before going on.

2.   Alternatively, this can mean *meet someone suddenly and quite unexpectedly*:

I ran into old Hawkins, our music master, the other day at the antiques fair – and he remembered me!

Who should I run into while on safari in Tanzania but my next-door neighbours!

Come across

This is a matter of finding something when you are *not* looking for it; that is, *the finding is accidental*:

I came across this old photograph in my bureau the other day, while I was turning the drawers out.

Discover

For things, this verb refers to finding something *whose existence was previously unknown*:

The planet Pluto was discovered long after the nearer ones.

For people, it emphasises both that a search is on and that the person was *behaving furtively or suspiciously:*

The fugitive was discovered hiding in a church.

Locate

Although this verb has other meanings, the one that interests us here is: *find the exact place or position*, when the object is known and we also know the general area to be searched:

We knew that the noise was coming from somewhere in the house, but it took us ages to locate it – in the loft.

It was known roughly where the galleon had sunk, so locating it was not difficult, but for years the great depth rendered the wreck impossible to reach.

Detect

Familiar from "detective", here we *use skill* to **detect** something important when it is hidden among other things:

The tax inspectors examining the company's books detected the existence of undeclared accounts in Switzerland.

The larvae of this butterfly are so perfectly camouflaged that they are almost impossible to detect among the leaves of the geranium.

48 FIT ~ SUIT

Fit

This is a matter of *physical shape or size*: whether an object has the right shape and/or size to enter a certain space without difficulty (often made clearer by adding *into*), or whether something will combine well with a situation:

> *The key fitted (into) the keyhole.*
> It entered, so it was apparently the right one for that lock.

> *The hat looked large, but when he tried it on, to his surprise it fitted perfectly.*
> The hat was the exact size for his head.

Suit

1. This is a question of *harmony and taste*: whether an object looks right in a certain situation:

   > *It just wouldn't suit a plump woman like me to wear slacks – I'm much too broad-hipped.*

   > *Her new hat suited her admirably because it didn't make her look elderly, like her previous ones.*

2. It is also a matter of *convenience*: whether something we are trying to arrange is a good time or moment for both people:

   > *If two o'clock is early for a meeting, would three suit you better?*

49 FLOOR ~ STOREY

Floor

This is the *base of a room* (any kind of room) – the flat part we stand and walk on and put our furniture on:

> *The Robinsons have had beautiful parquet floors laid in every room of their new house.*

The lowest floor of any building is the Ground Floor, which is at street level. In Britain this one is not included in numbering the floors of a building, so the First Floor is the one immediately above the Ground Floor, etc.:

> *We'll take the lift. We're only going to the First Floor, but with all this luggage it would be too tiring to walk up.*

Storey (old spelling: story)

This is an architectural notion. It constitutes one section of a building, from ceiling to floor and including all the rooms, so it is a way of *dividing the building into all its horizontal parts*, from the roof down to ground level:

> *If a building in this town is less than five storeys high, a lift is not compulsory, as having to walk up four floors is not considered excessive.*

50 FULL ~ SHEER ~ UTTER

Full

Apart from its familiar meaning of *leaving no empty space* in some kind of container, **full** can be used before concrete nouns to mean *complete* and before abstract nouns such as awareness or determination with the sense of "total":

> *He gave as full an answer as he could to the question.*
>
> *I started on the work in the full knowledge that I should not be able to finish it before dusk.*

Fully, the corresponding adverb, behaves similarly:

> *He answered the question as fully as he could.*
>
> *I started the job, knowing fully well (full well) that it was going to be highly problematic.*

Sheer and **Utter**

Basically, these both *mean total* or *nothing less than*. Both are used with nouns that describe:

a. *excesses of feeling*, such as joy, rapture, amazement, or loathing:

> *It would be sheer/utter bliss to be sitting in front of a warm fire again!*
>
> *Their faces revealed utter/sheer horror.*

b. *extreme characteristics or situations*, with the following difference:

1. **Sheer** can be used for both positive and negative kinds of extremity:

   > *We were astounded at the sheer perfection of it.*
   >
   > *It was sheer stupidity that caused him to fail.*

2. **Utter** is likely to be used more for *negative* cases (such as agony, misery, carelessness, or incompetence):

   > *The accident was due to the driver's utter recklessness.*
   >
   > *In view of the utter futility of their efforts, the rescuers had no option but to recall the helicopter and watch helplessly while the avalanche buried the mountaineers' bodies.*

This difference exists because **utter**, being slightly stronger, is marginally more dramatic.

(**Sheer** has other meanings besides this one, and you ought to look them up in a dictionary).

Utterly, similarly, is used in the same cases as the adjective:

- with very extreme and negative situations:

  > *It would be utterly ridiculous to complain now.*

- or to describe extreme emotional reactions:

  > *We were utterly taken aback to hear how ill he had been.*
  >
  > *When they had gone she found the bathroom in an utterly disgusting state.*

(Also see **Plenty, Full**)

51 GATHER ~ COLLECT ~ ACCUMULATE ~ ASSEMBLE

These verbs often change meaning according to whether they are transitive or intransitive, so it is necessary to examine them all in these two forms.

The intransitive use

Gather

People and certain animals **gather**; they come together out of curiosity or, in the case of animals, to participate in some way:

> *A crowd had soon gathered round the quarrelling drunks, watching them in amusement.*

> *Whales gather to mate at specific times of the year and in certain areas of the sea.*

> *All the members of the tribe gather for the proclamation of a new chief and the celebration that always follows.*

Collect

Quantities of very small objects **collect**, creating a mass of often-unwanted material:

> *Dust had collected in every corner of the closed room.*

> *So many dead leaves have collected in the drainpipe that it has become blocked.*

> *Where a slow river curves, sand tends to collect on the outside of the bend, leading to the formation of a strand.*

Accumulate

Problematic things **accumulate** – that is, they increase in number – when they cannot be dealt with at the right time:

> *My work accumulated alarmingly while I was away ill.*

Assemble

People **assemble** for meetings at which important matters have to be discussed:

Word went round that all the local people were to assemble in the village hall that evening to debate the issue.

The transitive use

Gather

People **gather** things with their hands:

A poor man came in sight, gathering winter fuel.

The planting had been done by the men, but the harvest was gathered by the women.

Collect

People **collect** objects that interest them, creating . **collections,** which sometimes become very valuable later:

The owner of the shop on the corner might be interested in those volumes; I know he collects certain kinds of books.

But **collect** can also be used for one object, with the meaning of *fetch*:

I'll collect the car when you tell me it's ready.

Accumulate

People **accumulate** non-material things such as wealth or financial problems, sometimes unintentionally:

He was a born gambler and accumulated so many debts at poker that his father had to intervene.

Assemble

Various *methods* exist to **assemble** people when a meeting is needed:

Ralph used blasts on his conch shell to assemble the boys.

Remember that **assemble** also means *put the parts together*:

This is the part of the factory where the cars are finally assembled.

· **52** GOLD/GOLDEN ~ GILT ~ SILVER/SILVERY ~ LEAD/LEADEN ~ BRASS/BRAZEN ~ WOOD/WOODEN ~ WOOL/WOOLLEN

At one time the two words in each of these pairs could not possibly be confused because the first was always a noun while the second was its adjective, so an object made of gold, for instance, was described as "golden". Later on, however, these nouns (all names of materials) came to be used as adjectives too, and this gave rise to a subtle change in the meaning of each second word. Let's examine these one by one.

Gold

We use this adjective for things made of this metal:

Wedding rings are sometimes made of platinum, but gold rings are the most popular.

He was given a gold watch when he retired from the office.

Golden

This is a poetic way of describing anything that has a *colour resembling gold* but is *not* made of that metal, for example: the sky at sunrise, a head of blond hair, a field of ripe wheat, etc.:

The rising sun illuminated the clouds with a rich golden light.

Gilt

If an object is *coated with a thin layer of gold paint* (as picture frames often are) the paint is called *gilt* and the object is described as **gilt** or is said to have been *gilded*:

The gilt frame round the engraving was worth more than the picture itself.

Silver

Also the adjective for the metal:

The basin of the fountain was covered with silver coins thrown in by romantic tourists.

Silvery

As with **golden,** this describes the *colour of silver* but not the actual metal and is used – again, poetically – for moonlight, for grey or white hair, and so on:

The silvery scales of the fishes in the tank flashed each time they turned.

Lead

As with **gold**:

The use of lead water pipes, once normal in domestic plumbing, is now strictly prohibited for health reasons.

Leaden

This is used in two ways: for anything of *a dull grey tone*, such as a heavily clouded sky, and also for things that are *metaphorically very heavy* – for instance the feet of somebody who has to walk in a certain direction but is almost too terrified to move:

With set face and leaden feet the prisoner took the last few steps to the execution block.

Brass

As with **gold**; but it can mean either the metal alloy itself or its colour:

When I was little, I loved the big brass knobs on the end of my bed.

Brazen

This time what is described is not a colour but a *defiantly impudent attitude or behaviour*, no doubt on account of the traditional brightness and hardness of brass:

She brazenly asserted she had prepared the whole meal without help, which was clearly impossible.

Wood

Nowadays this is the adjective for anything made of that substance:

They built up a beautiful wood fire and the room was soon gloriously warm.

Wooden

Although still sometimes used for things made of wood, such as furniture, this is equally common for a *stiff, unnatural, inexpressive manner*:

> *A good comedian can keep his audience in fits with an utterly wooden, unchanging expression on his face all the time.*

Woollen (US woolen)

This is the only one of these adjectives that is still regularly used in its original sense: for something made of wool:

> *You'd find woollen gloves far warmer than those leather ones you're wearing, you know.*

53 GRATEFUL ~ GRATIFIED ~ THANKFUL ~ THANKLESS

Grateful

This expresses straightforward *gratitude*. That is, we show our thanks for some kind or helpful action:

> *In the making of this film we are most grateful for all the assistance we have received from the people of this village.*

The negative is "ungrateful" and its noun is "ingratitude".

Gratified

It expresses pleasure and gratitude too, but this time we are *surprised*, not having expected it, and the feeling is not directed at anyone in particular. It is generally followed by an infinitive:

> *Harry was gratified to see that his ex–colleagues still remembered him and were pleased to see him.*

It has no equivalent abstract noun.

Thankful (noun: **thankfulness**)

This, surprisingly, does not mean a simple "thank you", because it is used in cases where nobody has done anything to deserve gratitude. Instead, it embodies a strong element of *relief* that the situation has improved or that the worst has not happened:

> *How thankful we were to see our destination at last, after all the hardships of the journey.*

> *He went in and walked quietly back to his desk, thankful that nobody seemed to have noticed his absence.*

Thankless

This is not the opposite of **thankful**, but is used to describe tasks, not people's feelings. A thankless task is one for which *we feel we receive no thanks* – and probably do not in reality receive any:

> *Mother always says that housework is a thankless job; other members of the family are quite happy to see it done but nobody shows any gratitude!*

54 HAPPY ~ UNHAPPY ~ SAD ~ CHEERFUL ~ PLEASED ~ GLAD

Happy

It describes the quality of life when it is *troublefree*, or the state of mind when a person is *free from suffering* and shows this in his facial expression and in his behaviour towards others:

> *Their later years were very happy ones: they had a lovely home, enjoyed good health, and loved each other dearly.*

> *Money does not necessarily make us happy; it brings plenty of worries, too.*

It can also describe a *strongly positive reaction* to something new:

> *Our friends in the camp were very happy to see us again and came crowding round to hear our news.*

Unhappy

It is simply the opposite case: the person, or his life, is not free of worries or troubles:

> *Although her parents know she has made an unhappy marriage, as long as she refuses to confide in them there is nothing they can do to help her.*

Sad

It describes either the expression on the face of somebody who is *regretful or cannot find enjoyment,* or a case where we see that *matters are not the best*:

> *It strikes me that a lot of these medieval saints merely look sad when the artist intended them to look pious!*

> *It's a sad business, all this reported corruption in the local authority.*

Cheerful

It describes an *attitude* shown by people who either have no serious troubles or don't let those troubles depress them:

> *Our milkman's a cheerful fellow: he always smiles and waves goodbye when he leaves. You'd never think he lost his wife only a month ago.*

Pleased

It is another positive reaction to a new circumstance, but in this case because the person *benefits in some way*:

> *My grandchildren are invariably pleased to see me: they know that I always bring them something!*

> *Maureen didn't look pleased when we turned up. I suspect she had been hoping to have a quiet afternoon on her own.*

Glad

Nowadays it is almost always followed by an infinitive, and it is not – unfortunately for poets – the opposite of **sad**. It displays *relief rather than pleasure or happiness*:

> *It had been a long, tiring day, and we were glad just to get home and take our shoes off.*

55 HINT ~ IMPLY ~ INTIMATE ~ INSINUATE

All these verbs refer to the transfer of information in such an indirect, inexplicit way that the message is not easily understood and often has to be guessed.

Hint

This is the most indirect way of transmitting a message, yet it can be immediately clear. This is because the words are usually accompanied by a facial expression or a movement of the body and a special tone of voice that show the hearer very exactly what is meant. In fact, a **hint** is often made completely without words. (If only words are used, the message can be baffling). When the **hint** leaves no doubt as to its meaning, we call it a **strong hint**:

> *"Is there a window open?" she asked with a little shiver, hinting clearly that someone should do something about it.*

Imply and Intimate

There is almost no difference in meaning when these refer to communicating information, although perhaps **imply** is a little more direct:

> *His brief comment implied that something had gone wrong, and I could hardly wait for a chance to speak to him in private to find out the facts.*

> *They intimated their support for my cause, so I did not need to ask for it openly.*

However, **imply** can be used of impersonal situations too, in the sense of *leading to something different*:

> *A change of government usually implies a change of policy.*

Insinuate

This verb has a strong suggestion of unworthy motives:

> *Without saying it openly, she insinuated that he had been helping himself to the club's funds.*

56 HISTORIC ~ HISTORICAL

Historical

Let's begin with **historical.** We use this for anything that has actually occurred and forms *part of history* – it is therefore a reality in the past, not something mythical, imaginary, or theoretical:

> *Thanks to the tenacity of Heinrich Schliemann, the Troy of legend is now recognised as a historical reality.*

Historic

We use this word for occurrences in the past that made *a singular impact on the world* – subsequently, if not at the time they happened – and are remembered for it:

> *The landing on the moon is regarded as one of Man's most historic achievements.*

57 HOLDING
(with pressure)

Very often, when we hold something there is a risk that we may drop it or lose it somehow. In that case we use pressure (of the hand or whatever part of the body we are using) to make sure it cannot escape. The following verbs express various ways of applying that pressure.

CLASP ~ CLENCH ~ CLING ~ GRIP

Clasp

1. To fit the fingers of both hands together:

> *Clasping his hands together to make a support, Jim told Ann to put one foot on them so that he could heave her up to reach the kitten in the tree.*

2.   To hold another person's hand very firmly:

> *As we stepped off the winning boat, the crowd pressed round us, cheering and clasping our hands with enthusiasm.*

3.   To put both arms (or legs) tightly round something:

> *Even with her infant clasped to her back, the mother ape can travel freely many miles through the jungle.*

Clench

Used for the fists or for the teeth, when we press either of these very tightly together:

> *The bigger boy clenched his fists threateningly and dared me to hit him first.*
>
> *Inserting a strip of coloured paper between my teeth, the dentist asked me to clench them and rub them against each other.*

Cling

To hold on very tightly to something, using as much of our body as we can. For plants, this describes the tight pressure of one plant against another when the first cannot stand alone:

> *From the helicopter the rescue team detected a child clinging desperately to a tree branch, with the floodwaters swirling only inches beneath her.*
>
> *Being too weak to support itself, this plant puts out tendrils that, by clinging to the host tree, enable the parasite to reach the sunlight many metres above.*

Grip

To press or close parts of the body (mostly the hands) on an object so tightly that it cannot slip or fall:

> *My daughter gripped my hand in panic as the boat started to turn over.*
>
> *Watch how the mother cat grips its young between its teeth and carries them to a safer place without hurting them.*

58 -IC / -ICAL ENDINGS

The basic rule to know whether to write *-ic* or *-ical* is simple enough: if there is already a noun ending in *-ic*, the corresponding adjective adds *-al*, as in:

Noun	*Adjective*
logic	logical
rhetoric	rhetorical
arithmetic	arithmetical
music	musical
a statistic	statistical
a cynic	cynical
a mystic	mystical

If there is no noun ending in *-ic*, then it is the adjective that has this ending, as in:

Noun	*Adjective*
basis	basic
drama	dramatic
tragedy	tragic
poetry	poetic
emphasis	emphatic
romance	romantic
fantasy	fantastic
system	systematic
optimist	optimistic

The adverbs for all these regularly, although illogically, end in *-ically*.

But of course there are complications: for instance quite often both forms are accepted, and there are many exceptions to the rule, as below:

1. Remember that nouns ending in *-ic* frequently behave like adjectives, and in such a case, we don't add *-al* to them:

   An arithmetic class = a class in which arithmetic is taught.

   A music hall = a hall built for performing music in.

2. When subjects of *educational study* end in *-ics*, this same form becomes the adjective when referring to those subjects (a mathematics teacher, a physics examination).

3. **Public** is both noun (the public) and adjective (public relations).

4. The adjective for **Bible** is *biblical*.

5. **Magic** (noun) has two adjectives: *magic,* meaning that something has unnatural origins or qualities, and *magical*, which has a similar meaning to *wonderful*:

   The sorcerer uttered some magic words and the wall opened.

   Twilight gives the lake a magical quality that cannot be described.

6. **Politics** gives us *political*, but from *policy* we get *politic*, which means *prudent* or *expedient*:

   Her political views clashed with those of her family and caused endless arguments.

   It would not be politic to grant any concessions to the strikers without some kind of guarantee of good faith.

7. **Electric** alludes to things that consist largely of electricity, that function with electricity, or in which it is the electricity that counts:

   An electric current = a movement of electrons.

   An electric motor = a motor that runs on electricity.

   Electric light = light created by an electric current.

   An electric storm = one in which electric flashes are produced.

   Electrical is used for anything associated with electric apparatus:

   An electrical engineering course.

8. With the noun **irony** we have a choice: both *ironic* and *ironical* are used.

9. The adjective for **geography** is generally *geographic* in the USA but is more likely to be *geographical* in Britain.

10. The adjective of **myth** is *mythical*, not *mythic*.

11. **Catholic** is both a common noun and the adjective of Catholicism:

    Being a Roman Catholic means accepting the dogmas of the Catholic Church.

12. Not all nouns that end in *-ist* form their adjectives with *-istic*, like *optimist* (above); sometimes the *-ist* serves for both noun and adjective alike, especially where religion or politics are involved (Buddhist, Socialist, etc.)

(For **Classic, Classical**; **Historic, Historical** and **Economic, Economical**, see separate entries).

59 JUST ~ ONLY

Occasionally these words have the same meaning, but in most cases there is quite a difference: **just** can mean either *merely* or *exactly* while **only** never means anything but *no more ... than*. Besides, **just** can be used in distinctive structural ways that are impossible for **only**. Here are the main differences between the two words.

Just

This is the usual word before an *imperative*, where its effect is to *soften the order* by stressing that the action wanted is not difficult or unreasonable:

On the telephone: *"Just hold the line a moment, please"*.

Just is very much used to refer to *relative time*, especially the immediate past or future, and the tenses it appears in are mostly the Perfect and the Continuous:

We've just been talking to your uncle about it.

Just, *used before a verb of feeling,* (in one of the simple tenses) serves to intensify that verb:

> *Sylvia just hates the smell of horses.*

Similarly, **just,** *before a modal auxiliary,* emphasizes it:

> *She just couldn't see what I meant.*

Just, before other expressions, often means *exactly* or *precisely*:

> *So, you're Janet? You're just the person I wanted to see!*
>
> *Just as the clock struck twelve, the lights all went out.*

Only

Even when the two words seem to mean the same thing, there is a difference: **only** has a *restrictive* function, adding seriousness and importance, while **just** is used in exactly the opposite way – to show that the situation is *not important or serious*:

> *He lives only two doors away, so there's no excuse for not going to see him.*
>
> *He lives just two doors away, so we're always bumping into him.*

Alternatively we could say that **only** is *pessimistic* in sense while **just** is *optimistic*:

> *There's only room for one; we'll have to wait.*
>
> *There's just room for one more, so jump in!*

If the speaker describes *an action* with **just**, he thinks of it as normal and unimportant; if with **only**, he is speaking defensively:

> *He just smiled at me and went out.*
>
> *Don't look so worried: I was only joking!*

The combination **only just** with a simple tense means that something *nearly didn't happen*; in other cases it reinforces the meaning of **just**:

> *They only just caught the train after all.*
>
> *What! Going out again! But you've only just come in!*

Finally, remember that **just** is very colloquial as well as idiomatic and a lot *depends on the tone of the voice*, which means that in writing, where the stress and intonation cannot be shown, its use easily becomes ambiguous, so a good writer handles it with great care.

60 JUST
(used with tenses)

He's just come in ~ He just came in.

You are unlikely to hear the first of these phrases in the United States, but both are used in British English – with a significant difference of meaning.

He's just come in

This **just**, used with the Present Perfect Tense, has the effect of indicating *recentness*: he came in only moments ago, so he is here now, as he hasn't had time to leave again.

He just came in

Although this is the normal way of describing recentness in the US, in British English **just** used like this with a simple tense has no connection with time at all; it shows *natural-seeming behaviour*. Here, the tense used (the Past Simple) indicates an action that occurred at a certain point in the past, and **just** has the meaning of *simply* or *merely*. What is implied in this case is that he was not expected – or he was lucky not to have been challenged or stopped at the entrance. In other words, **just** throws *great emphasis on the sense of the verb*.

Special points to note:

1. In many situations **he just (+ a past tense)**, stresses either the *astonishing simplicity of an action* or a surprising *lack of emotion* in the doer:

   > *He just walked in.*
   > This means that nobody stopped him or that he did not need to enter in any more spectacular way.

I don't worry about other people's opinions of me; I just say what I think, and if they don't like it, that's too bad!
The doer feels no responsibility for his behaviour.

He just shrugged the incident off.
He didn't show the shock or alarm that might have been expected.

2.   In negative situations, the implication is that the doer *feels (or felt) under no obligation* to behave as expected:

I just didn't care whether I had offended her or not.

He just won't get up when I call him.

61 KIND ~ KINDLY

Both **kind** and **kindly** are adjectives, and there is also the adverb **kindly**. Let's examine the adjectives first.

Kind

This describes two possible things: *the nature of a person* or *an action performed.*

1.   A **kind** person is one who thinks of the welfare of others and tries to help without waiting to be asked. We can call that person **kind** because we have had experience of this kindness on previous occasions:

You'll find the staff at the clinic very kind: they're always ready to listen to people's troubles and lend a hand if they can.

2.   A **kind** action is one that is well meant and is intended to help but is very often not expected:

When we came back from holiday last week, our flight was delayed several hours and we got home too late to buy anything for supper, but our next-door neighbours at once invited us in to share theirs, which we thought was extremely kind of them.

Kindly (adjective)

1. Although very similar to **kind** in form, when referring to people, this describes a person's *apparent nature* (the impression we have):

    > *The traffic policeman had a kindly look about him, so I went up to him and asked him the way.*

2. When referring to actions, the difference from **kind** is less clear, for **kindly** also implies spontaneity but stresses the *intention rather than the results*:

    > *Seeing how pale Alison had turned, the woman sitting beside her made the kindly gesture of fanning her vigorously with a magazine.*

Kindly (adverb)

Here too there are two uses:

1. The adverbial form of the adjective **kind** *to describe helpfulness in an action*:

    > *The bank clerk kindly filled the form in for me, although I suppose I could easily have done it.*

2. The special pre-verb adverb used *before an imperative* verb, or after *will...*, or in the middle of an infinitive (in indirect requests) as a more respectful form of *please...*:

    > Notice in museum: *Kindly leave all cameras at the desk.*

    > Hotel notice: *Will guests kindly vacate their rooms by 12 midday.*

    > *They asked us to kindly come back later.*

But quite often the speaker feels *impatience, anger, or scorn*, and the result sounds sarcastic:

> *Jimmy, kindly stop making that noise immediately! If I've told you once, I've told you a hundred times!*

> *Will you kindly leave me alone! I know what I'm doing!*

> *Tell your brother to kindly put his disagreement in writing if he feels that strongly about it!*

62 KNOWN

Known as

People, places, and things are sometimes given a name that is different from the original or correct one. (In the case of persons we call this a "nickname"). For example, the Bank of England has been described by the citizens of London as the "Old Lady of Threadneedle Street". In such a case we say that that person or thing is **known as** (whatever is its nickname):

> *The Roman emperor Caius was known popularly as Caligula.*
>
> *To the local population, the Mississippi is known as Old Man River.*

Known to + infinitive verb

But if we want to say that *a fact is known*, we use the phrase **known to + infinitive verb.**

> *Jericho is known to be the oldest surviving city in the world.*
>
> *Her mother was known to have a fondness for handsome men!*
>
> *The Arabs are known to have invented a symbol for zero.*
>
> *The planet Jupiter is known to possess rings like those of Saturn, although they are invisible from Earth.*

Known for

This phrase means that a person or a place has a reputation for a particular quality or characteristic:

> *This artist is better known for his paintings than for his sculptures.*
>
> *The English are not well known for good cooking.*
>
> *Salamanca is known all over the world for its university and for the harmonious beauty of its buildings.*

63 LAST ~ LATEST ~ FINAL ~ ULTIMATE

Last

With this adjective, what interests us is that:

1. *The series appears to have stopped*:

   The last time he wrote was some ten years ago, and we haven't heard anything since then.

2. *There are, or will be, no more*:

   In my country the last day of the week is Saturday, not Sunday.

   Her last book was written only months before her death.

   This is the last job I'm going to do before I retire.

Latest

This refers to the last of a series to appear, although *more are expected*:

Have you seen his latest play? If he writes more like this he will soon become very famous.

Final

This means last, too; after all the others comes this one. But there is *a stronger suggestion of termination*; there will definitely be no more:

This is my final offer. Accept it now or you'll regret it for the rest of your life!

Ultimate

This can mean not only last but *separated from the preceding ones by a great distance*. It is the one we reach after a very long time and no more are considered, so it is often the one least expected:

The farthest of all these remote galaxies must represent the ultimate extent of the Universe.

It can also mean a *culmination*: the final development in a general trend – the most satisfactory or the most complete:

> *It should not be supposed that humanity is nature's ultimate creation; there are likely to be many new species in the distant future.*

64 LAUGHING ~ SMILING

The basic distinction between these actions is that **laughing** is a (noisy) reaction to a new situation whilst **smiling** is a display of emotion, shown by facial movement.

Ways of Laughing

CACKLE ~ CHORTLE ~ CHUCKLE ~ GIGGLE ~ GUFFAW ~ SNIGGER ~ TITTER

Cackle

The high-pitched way very old people laugh, strongly reminiscent of a noise made by hens:

> *The crone's comments left us totally perplexed, and seeing this she shut the door cackling loudly.*

Chortle

To laugh suddenly and rather explosively, as some middle-aged men do, with great amusement. The sound is more "Ho, ho" than "Ha, ha":

> *My uncle chortled when he recalled the disastrous mistake he had made on his wedding day.*

Chuckle

To laugh quietly to oneself, especially when reading or remembering something funny:

> *Janet was reading the Sunday paper and evidently finding it entertaining, to judge from her chuckling.*

Giggle

To laugh irrepressibly (and therefore for some time) at something that other people wouldn't find amusing or at moments when laughing at all is considered out of place. This is very characteristic of adolescents.

Children are liable to giggle when they are embarrassed.

Guffaw

To laugh very loudly and coarsely, usually at something perhaps indelicate, that not everyone would find funny:

He must have been telling them about his adventures in the girls' dormitory, because he had his friends guffawing uproariously.

Snigger

This is the way people laugh when they know they shouldn't; the sound is half-smothered, usually indicating shame:

The boys were sniggering at the scenes of nudity in the magazine.

Titter

To laugh in a silly, nervous or embarrassed fashion, especially when circumstances are wrong for laughter:

He was a self-educated man, this new teacher, and he made the class titter every time he pronounced "hyperbole" as "hyper-bowl".

Ways of Smiling

BEAM ~ GRIN ~ SIMPER ~ SMIRK

Beam

To smile broadly, with great pleasure or satisfaction:

We were welcomed enthusiastically by the beaming hotel proprietor, who had not seen a guest for two weeks.

Grin

Also to smile broadly, but in this case there may be no obvious reason – it may show silent personal amusement, but sometimes it is merely indicative of stupidity!

> *Jimmy, do stop grinning like that! What's funny about trying to mend a puncture when you haven't got the right tools?*

Simper

To smile self-consciously or affectedly:

> *The great man winked broadly at the woman behind the bar, making her blush and simper.*

Smirk

Here a person smiles when he is pleased with himself or with what he has done. To others it looks pointless or silly:

> *By the way he was smirking, I knew he had done something to annoy me.*

65 LAY ~ LIE

These two verbs appear in practically all books that deal with problems in English, but so many people (English-speakers on both sides of the Atlantic as well as foreigners) confuse them that it is never unnecessary to repeat the difference between them.

The essential difference is that **lay** can be both transitive and intransitive while **lie** is only intransitive. This means that **lie** can never take an object.

Lay – Laid – Laid

This verb has three meanings:

1. To place (or build) something horizontally;
2. To deposit (used only for eggs);

3. To put all the required objects on a dining table, ready for starting a meal.

The first of these is obviously the most important, and the things we most often **lay** (or, in the passive, that are most often laid) are things that have a flat shape: a hand or hands, a book or document, a human body, a floor (that is, the tiles that make up a floor), etc.:

> *I think we should lay him on the sofa until he recovers.*
>
> *Instructions for taking an oath: Lay your hand on the Book and repeat after me ...*
>
> *To her astonishment he laid his head on her shoulder, sighed deeply, and went to sleep.*
>
> *Clean towels had been laid out for us on the bed.*
>
> *A new pipeline is to be laid from the port right across the country.*

And here are examples of the two other uses:

> *Turtles come out of the sea to lay their eggs, which they do after scraping a hole in a beach.*
>
> *Oh dear, lunch is all ready to serve up and the table hasn't even been laid!*

Lie (the irregular verb: **Lie – Lay – Lain**)

This means simply one of these three cases:

1. To have fallen:

> *He was found lying face down beside the overturned vehicle.*
>
> *There was a deep hollow where the column had lain.*
>
> *That log has been lying there so long that ants have made a nest under it.*

2. To position oneself horizontally (usually with "down"), for things that are relatively *tall* (long vertically) and can change position; that is, living creatures like persons or animals:

> *Now lie still and go to sleep, you naughty little girl!*
>
> *At a word from its master the dog lay down at his feet.*

3. To be already in a horizontal position, for things that are *flat* (papers, books, towns, countries, land, etc.):

   Books and magazines were lying all over the floor.

   Tibet lies between India and China.

   The village lay in a hollow between steep hills.

66 LIFE ~ LIVING ~ LIVELIHOOD

Life

This word, with which we use the verb "to live" or (better) "to lead", can refer to several things:

1. Our mere *biological existence*:

   A matter of life or death.

2. The *period of time* between birth and death:

   She enjoyed a much longer life than her husband did.

3. The accumulation of *events and experiences* that happen to the individual:

   I can say I have had a very rich life.

   Life is full of surprises, you know.

4. The particular *way each person chooses to live*:

   He led a life of luxury while the money lasted.

5. Any living thing or all living things considered together:

   There is no immediate sign of life in the desert.

   Is there life on any other planet, I wonder?

Living

Again, there are several meanings:

1. The *action* of leading one's life:

    Dying seems easier than living in such cases.

2. The *action of occupying a home*:

    I hated living in that tiny house.

3. The *cost of day-to-day survival* (used with "to earn" or "to make"):

    He earned his living by repairing shoes.

    He made a living by repairing shoes.

Livelihood

There's only one meaning in modern English that is worth noting – *the money necessary for our daily needs*, so it is the same as 3. above:

> *His livelihood had always depended on his cunning rather than on his talents, for he was an expert swindler.*

67 LIGHT EFFECTS

English is rich in words that express various manifestations of light, whether the kind of light emitted from the source or the effects of it on other surfaces. It is worth remembering that most of these can be used very effectively in a figurative sense, too, and examples of this possibility are included, where appropriate.

Here is a list of light-effect words in alphabetic order. (Unless otherwise stated, the same word serves for both verb and noun).

BLAZE ~ DAZZLE ~ FLARE ~ FLASH ~ FLICKER ~ FLOODLIGHT ~ GLEAM ~ GLIMMER ~ GLINT ~ GLISTEN ~ GLITTER ~ GLOSS ~ GLOW ~ ILLUMINATE ~ SCINTILLATE ~ SHEEN ~ SHIMMER ~ SHINE ~ SPARKLE ~ TWINKLE

Blaze

An intense light, frequently accompanied by great heat, caused by either a fierce conflagration or a high-powered electrical element:

> *The blaze from the burning paint factory could be seen for miles around.*

> *The fierce red light from the blazing forest fire illuminated the sky, night after night, for over a week.*

> *His eyes blazed with uncontrollable anger.*

Dazzle

The light in our eyes is so strong that we cannot see anything for some time afterwards:

> *I was so dazzled by the spotlight that the audience was completely invisible to me.*

> *When she was introduced to the film star, she was so dazzled that she couldn't think of anything to say to him.*

Flare

Also an intense light, but of short duration and perhaps without heat. As a noun it often refers to a kind of light signal released high in the air:

> *Ships in distress shoot brilliant lights called flares into the sky to attract attention.*

> *Pouring petrol on a fire will make it flare but will not create much heat.*

> *Trouble has flared up again in the Caucasus region.*

Flash

A sudden bright but very short-lived light, such as is caused by atmospheric electricity or a short-circuit. This word is also used for the familiar electrical instrument that adds light when photographing:

> *You'll need a flash for your camera if you want to take a good picture indoors.*

> *His glasses flashed in the bright sunlight whenever he turned his head.*

I had a sudden flash of inspiration and knew exactly how to deal with the problem.

Flicker

For a flame, an unsteady movement in the light emitted; for a lamp, an abnormal and irritating pulsation:

There was a brief flicker from the match, and then it went out, leaving us in the dark again.

When a candle begins to flicker and smoke, it means that the wick needs trimming.

Scientists say that the high-speed flicker of a fluorescent tube is very harmful to the eyes.

The committee showed little more than a flicker of interest in the project, so it now looks like being forgotten again.

Floodlight

To illuminate a large area or the entire surface of a building. The noun for this is "floodlighting":

The cathedral is floodlit every night during the summer.

Gleam

Large dirtfree surfaces can reflect light to a certain extent without having been specially prepared or polished:

A distant gleam of water showed them that they were getting near the lake.

She had just dusted the furniture and the wood now gleamed gratefully.

Some of the women declare they saw a distinct gleam of triumph in her eyes as she left the church on her new husband's arm.

Glimmer

How a light looks when it is very faint or is seen from a great distance:

A glimmer round the bend ahead of us told us that we were nearing the end of the tunnel.

A lantern glimmering in one of the upper windows of the inn was the signal the smugglers out at sea had been waiting for.

Glint

A flashing form of light from distant or very small objects, especially if they are metallic:

We saw a metallic glint among the grains of river sand and knew that we had found gold.

The speartips of the advancing army glinted on the distant hillside.

The pirates' eyes glinted with excitement as the old coffer was opened.

Glisten

It describes the way a wet surface, such as the skin of a bather emerging from the water, shines with each movement:

His face was flushed with the effort of pulling and his forehead glistened with sweat as he bent over the oars.

Glitter

A multitude of flashes from small surfaces each reflecting the light in turn, as in movement:

Christmas tree decorations provide a cheerful glitter as the tinsel sways with each tiny draught of air.

The sequins on her dress glittered in the candle-light.

Gloss (For the effects of light, only the noun is used)

The special shine on a surface produced by a polish, a varnish, or a protective coating on paper. The associated adjective is "glossy", as for book covers:

After you've worn new shoes for a couple of days they begin to lose their gloss.

The initial gloss of working for such an important company lasted only a week or two, as she found out how they treated their employees.

Glow

A shine from inside instead of only from the surface:

Despite the darkness, she could see where he was standing by the glow from his cigarette each time he drew on it.

A cat's eyes glow green in the dark.

Mother's face glowed with pride as our Albert went up to receive his award.

Illuminate (Verb only. The noun is "illumination")

To cast light on:

The rising sun had begun to illuminate the mountain top.

Enthusiasm illuminated his face as he showed me his invention.

Lustre (US luster) (noun)

A beautiful bright shine on a material:

The lustre on the horse's coat showed how well cared-for he was.

There's no lustre in always being second in command.

Scintillate (verb)

To emit small flashes of very bright light. But this verb is seldom used in the literal sense nowadays and when it does it almost always appears as the present participle used adjectivally:

His conversation was far from scintillating and we were soon thoroughly bored.

Sheen (noun)

Like **lustre**, it describes a beautiful shine, but especially on natural materials like fur or skin:

Her hair had that glorious sheen that only a first-class shampoo can produce.

Shimmer

Used either for the apparent up-and-down movement of distant surfaces on a very hot day or for the apparent movement of light on the surface of water:

The intense heat created a shimmer over the hills on the horizon, as if they were dancing.

Across the bay, the lights of the harbour shimmered on the ripples blown along by the night breeze.

Shine

The reflection of light from a clean or polished surface:

> *Advertisement: Regular use of this furniture cream will ensure that lasting shine you have always wanted.*
>
> *The sun shone brilliantly that morning in a pure blue sky.*
>
> *A really clever child will soon shine at school.*

Sparkle

Tiny flashes of light when there is movement, a characteristic most typically found in cut gems:

> *A chandelier's charm is the constant sparkle from its hundreds of glass facets.*
>
> *The reception was an occasion for immaculate uniforms and sparkling diamonds.*
>
> *As he lifted the glass over her head his eyes sparkled with mischief.*

Twinkle

Light shining in the intermittent way that we find typically in stars in northern latitudes:

> *The morning star was still twinkling faintly, low on the horizon in the dawn light.*
>
> *Every time I saw that twinkle in my uncle's eye, I knew he was pulling my leg.*

68 LIKE ~ AS

Often and easily confused, these two words can best be distinguished by their grammatical functions: when correctly used, **like** is only a *preposition*, whilst **as** is both *preposition and conjunction*. Let's study them in these roles:

Like (when a preposition)

It indicates only a *similarity, not a reality*:

> *Margarine is made to look like butter.*
> Margarine isn't really butter, but it looks like it.
>
> *They live like kings with the fortune they have inherited.*
> Of course, they are not actually kings.

When he's sober he's quite normal, but when he's drunk he behaves like a lunatic. He only resembles a lunatic.

Like you, I'm terribly fond of chocolate.

As (when a preposition)

This word describes *reality, however temporary,* and shows the (usually temporary) *function* of a person or object, the *job* that a person does, or the *role* in which we see someone:

> *He folded his jacket and used it as a pillow.* (= function).
>
> *She worked as a hotel cook during her vacation.* (= job).
>
> *I am speaking now as a friend, not as your doctor.* (= role).

It is particularly used with verbs of mental attitude, such as *regard, look on, think of, see (in the mind),* or *consider* (unless it shows opinion), and with *describe*:

> *We regard this house as our real home.*
>
> *They described the storm as the worst they had experienced.*
>
> *I am considering him as my possible successor.*

As (when a conjunction)

There are several uses of **as** in this form:

1. To offer *an explanation*, although possibly not the actual reason (to give a reason we use "because"):

   > *As it was a warm day, the windows were all open.*
   > Possibly this wasn't the only reason for opening all the windows, although it was a very logical one in the circumstances.
   >
   > *I called him Sir, as he looked old enough to be my father.*

2. To *comment on or stress the circumstances*. But a special characteristic of this structure is that **as** is followed by a verb *without a subject*. That is, it is followed only by the predicate, and it would be quite wrong to include any subject:

   > *Then the car stalled, as had so often happened before.*

As is common in this area, the local water is very hard.

She was late, as might have been expected.

3. In *elliptical phrases of comparison or comment*; that is, where the verb is understood but not visible:

    They argued in bed, as (they did) at work.

    As (had happened) previously, there was no clear result.

69 LIQUID MOVEMENT

As liquids move faster or more slowly according to their density and their freedom of movement, I have divided the following verbs into (relatively) fast and slow movements. You can assume that, unless otherwise specified, these verbs are used most for water, although the examples may include other kinds of liquids.

However, there is one basic verb to consider first:

Flow

This is the essential verb for all liquids. It shows that the liquid is moving in a certain direction but doesn't tell us *how* it moves:

Our blood flows round the entire body through the arteries and veins.

The Nile flows northwards from central Africa to the Mediterranean Sea.

Hot lava flowed down the volcano's side like a river of fire.

A glacier is a liquid, flowing infinitely slowly and carving a valley for itself as it moves.

Fast, Unimpeded Movements

POUR ~ GUSH ~ CASCADE ~ RUN ~ SPOUT ~ SPURT ~ SPRAY ~ SPLASH ~ SPATTER ~ SQUIRT ~ STREAM ~ FLOOD ~ SWIRL ~ WELL

(These are in order of sense, not in alphabetic order)

Pour

The liquid *passes very rapidly* along a defined course such as a riverbed or *emerges fast and smoothly* from a rather narrow source, such as a pipe:

> *Amy poured the old tea down the drain and washed the pot.*

> *As the farmer lifts the sluice gate, the water pours into the field.*

Gush

The liquid again emerges from a narrow source, but *with great force*, as if under pressure:

> *Red wine gushed from the wineskins as Don Quixote struck them.*

Cascade

The liquid comes *over the edge of something* (as in a cascade):

> *With both taps turned full on, the water had reached the brim of the bath-tub and was cascading onto the floor.*

Run

We use this only to describe the *route followed* by the liquid over a surface, so it is usually accompanied by a preposition of direction (down, into, along, etc.):

> *Rainwater from the roof collects in the guttering and then runs down drainpipes to the ground.*

Spout

The liquid emerges from a source so narrow (such as a spout) that *it travels horizontally* a short distance before beginning to fall. **Gush** can describe exactly the same movement, but then the emphasis is on the force rather than the direction:

> *With the force of his shaking, the stopper suddenly came off the bottle and the contents spouted all over him.*

Spurt

The liquid emerges with force, but *intermittently or repeatedly*:

> *From the way the blood spurted from the cut, I knew I had severed an artery, not a vein.*

Spray

This very familiar verb shows that the liquid comes out with great force but through such a small aperture that it is in the form of tiny droplets:

> *Spraying your roses is better than other anti-greenfly methods as it ensures that the insecticide reaches every part of the plant.*

Splash

The liquid is subjected to a violent movement that sends it flying through the air and hitting someone or something:

> *She tripped as she came in and some of the coffee she was carrying splashed the carpet.*

Spatter

(An older form is **bespatter**.) As with **splash**, the liquid comes with force and arrives in drops, but it is *often a dirty liquid* and there is less of it:

> *I was soon spattered with mud from passing vehicles.*

Squirt

The movement is restricted in such a way that the liquid comes out in a *single (often unexpected) direction*:

> *A simple mechanism presses against this valve as it turns, so the water squirts in a different arc each time, covering a greater area than is possible with traditional irrigation.*

> *Our favourite childhood game was to turn the tap full on and squirt the water over each other by pressing with one finger.*

Stream

Derived from the noun, this verb tells us that the movement is massive; it is a great amount of liquid *travelling fast and smoothly* in one direction:

> *He crawled out from under the overturned vehicle, with blood streaming from a terrible gash on his head.*

> *Film scenes invariably show rainy days with water absolutely streaming down the windows in the most unbelievable way.*

Flood

As the associated noun suggests, the movement is massive: it is a *relatively great volume* of liquid, but the more important aspect is *the area or surface covered*:

> *This river is notorious for flooding every spring, leaving many homes under water.*

> *The sea dykes broke under the strain and seawater flooded the polders.*

Swirl

The liquid *revolves quickly* in circles or half-circles:

> *I watched him swirling his brandy absentmindedly round and round in the glass.*

> *Why is it that, when you pull the plug out, the water tends to swirl in an anti-clockwise direction?*

Well

Adapted from the noun "well", this verb describes the fast outward movement of a liquid from below the surface:

> *As the surgeon made the first incision, dark red blood welled up from the cut.*

Slow (or Restricted) Movements

BUBBLE ~ TRICKLE ~ SEEP ~ OOZE ~ DRIP ~ SPILL ~ SLOP
(Not alphabetically listed)

Bubble

As the verb implies, the liquid emerges in the form of bubbles:

> *I have always been fascinated by champagne bubbling out of the bottle.*

Trickle

The liquid flows *in very small quantities*:

> *The heat in there was appalling: I could feel drops of sweat starting to trickle down my back.*

> *This cake will be greatly improved if you trickle some warm honey over it before serving.*

Seep

The liquid has to *pass through a material* such as cloth or plaster, which, although porous, greatly hampers the flow:

> *He had moved in his sleep and blood had seeped through the bandage, making a dark red stain.*

Ooze

The liquid is *so dense* that it can move only very slowly:

> *Oh, dear: there's a lot of black oil oozing out from under the car!*

Drip

The liquid runs down fine threads or hairs, or has to pass through such a tiny aperture that *it forms hanging drops*, which keep falling steadily:

> *Why don't you go and dry your hair? You're dripping it all over me!*

> *That tap kept me awake, dripping all night.*

Spill

As the container is transported or jerked, some of the contents *fall over the edge*:

> *Careful! You're spilling your coffee!*
>
> *If boiling milk spills, mop it up quickly before it dries.*

Slop

This is like **spill**, but with *more liquid coming over the edge* of the container, and for a longer period:

> *The rising wind began to slop water into our little boat.*
>
> *With each step it took, water slopped out of the bucket and ran down the donkey's leg.*

70 LITTLE ~ SMALL

While both words include the sense of reduced size, these are the differences between them:

Little

This, being a subjective adjective (the opposite of **big**), is almost a term of endearment: we use it of things (usually rather small things) for which we feel affection and towards which we may even feel protective. "Little" things and "little" people enchant us, although their size is often immaterial; in fact, to call something "dear little ..." doesn't necessarily mean that it is less than normal in size, but it does mean that we are fond of it.

For instance, a little child is one who is too young to be left alone for long; the little finger is the smallest (and weakest) one on the hand; and virtually everything that children enjoy hearing about in a fairy tale is little.

Small

Small does refer very explicitly to the size aspect, being the exact opposite of **large**, and it gives a purely objective description – few people would disagree with it.

Examples:

A mother will call her baby "little", but a neighbour (or a doctor, who is an impartial observer) might comment that the baby is "small" for its age.

However, there is another distinction that is well worth noting. **Little** is sometimes used in a very different way: to show anger or contempt:

"My son-in-law will have his little joke" said Mrs Greene acidly, obviously hurt by Harry's allusion to her age.

We can see this better when it follows a pejorative adjective such as "silly" or "nasty" (or "horrible" or "disgusting"):

Oh, those nasty little Robinson kids have been picking the flowers in our garden again!

71 LOOKING
(Ways of Looking)

Looking is a voluntary act: when we want to see something we turn our eyes towards it – we are looking at it. If we don't want to see it, we can turn our eyes away from it or close them. However, there are very many ways of looking, as below, in order of sense.

Looking with (or without) Attention

GLANCE ~ STARE ~ SCRUTINIZE~ CONTEMPLATE ~ REGARD ~ GAZE ~ WATCH ~ EYE ~ GAWP ~ GOGGLE

Glance

To look so briefly that you have no chance to see the thing well:

Too busy to pay much attention to the report, he only glanced at it on his way out of the room and had soon forgotten it existed.

Stare

To look *fixedly* (i.e. without moving the eyes away) at something, usually with surprise or interest, but sometimes with strong emotions such as alarm or horror:

> *I noticed everyone in the street staring at his strange garb and outlandish haircut.*

> *Everyone stared as she got to her feet and began to undress.*

Scrutinize

To examine something with *great attention*:

> *The lawyers scrutinized the document for a long time before agreeing that it was valid.*

Contemplate and Regard

To look steadily but with only moderate interest, often while thinking. We tend to use **contemplate** for objects or scenes and **regard** for other people:

> *The young journalist contemplated the scene of the catastrophe with awe, wondering how to begin his report.*

> *My father regarded me thoughtfully for a few moments before answering my question.*

Gaze

Also to look fixedly, but without really seeing what is in front of you because *you cannot think clearly or your thoughts are elsewhere*:

> *I gazed in horror at the examination sheet, wondering how on earth I could possibly answer so many questions in one hour.*

> *She spent the whole journey gazing out of the window while she tried to plan what to tell her parents.*

Watch

To look at *something that is moving*, like traffic, *or changing* in some way, even over a long period of time, like a child's development. The movement keeps our interest:

> *We stood there for several minutes, watching the sun go down in a red sky.*

Over the next ten years, she watched her village grow from a rural backwater into a thriving industrial town.

Eye

To look at something with *caution, suspicion or speculation*:

He eyed the package on his desk thoughtfully, wondering what it contained and where it had come from.

Gawp

To look with such astonishment or fascination that your *mouth falls open*:

The first time a motorcar appeared in the town, many years ago, the local people gawped incredulously; nowadays, on seeing vehicles, no-one turns to look twice.

Goggle

Like **gawp**, to look with *utter fascination*, but in this case with the eyes wide open, unable to look at anything else (the television set is often scornfully called "the goggle box"):

They absolutely goggled at the mass of tattoos that covered his chest and arms.

Looking from a Distance

SURVEY ~ SCAN ~ VIEW

Survey

To look at an object *from a certain distance in order to see it better and more completely*. Sometimes the intention is also to take measurements or make calculations:

Having finished the painting, I stood back to survey the results of so much work and to judge whether anything else needed doing.

Scan

To look at something large or finely detailed *from side to side*. In the case of texts or pictures this action has to be repeated progressively in order to cover the entire surface:

The ship's crew scanned the horizon for signs of land.

One of a sub-editor's jobs is to scan every article submitted to the newspaper in case it contains any "dangerous" elements. After that, he reads it slowly to assess its worth.

View

Like **survey**, this means looking from a certain distance, but usually *for the first time*, and there is consequently some kind of reaction:

He viewed the mess before him with dismay.

Looking with Difficulty

PEER ~ PEEP ~ SQUINT

Peer

Circumstances are unfavourable (it is dark, or your eyes are not good), so you have to *make an effort to see*, which often involves half-closing your eyes to increase the magnifying effect:

They peered through the smoke, trying to make out what had happened.

Even with my reading glasses on I had to peer hard at the bee to distinguish the special markings I had been told about.

Peep

To look *through a very small aperture or over a high obstacle*:

She was peeping at me from between partly opened fingers.

(A rather old-fashioned alternative verb is **peek**).

Squint

To look *from a difficult angle*, such as from one side, or when the light is not in a good position, which means that despite your efforts you cannot see the object at all well:

It was so close to my eyes that I could only squint at it.

Showing your Feelings with your Look

FROWN ~ GLARE ~ SCOWL ~ GLOWER ~ OGLE ~ LEER

Frown

To lower the eyebrows, perhaps to concentrate or to see better in strong light, as the eyebrows help to shade the eyes, or to show disapproval:

> *He frowned thoughtfully as he read her letter.*

> *When you frown like that I know you secretly disagree.*

Glare

To open the eyes very wide in great anger in order to frighten someone:

> *The farmer glared furiously at the campers.*

Scowl

To knit the eyebrows and *look hard in anger*:

> *Instead of apologising, he scowled silently at the teacher.*

Glower

A combination of **glaring** and **scowling** that shows *great anger or hatred that cannot be vented*:

> *The old man glowered in bitter fury at the soldiers as they set his home alight.*

Ogle

To use your eyes to indicate to someone that you find them very attractive:

> *He knew he was good-looking, but even so, the way the nurses ogled him was a source of embarrassment to him.*

Leer

To look at someone in an openly lascivious way, imagining, anticipating, or expecting sexual relations:

> *The workmen on the site turned to look hard as she passed, leering at her tight clothes and sinuous walk.*

72 LOUDNESS OF VOICE

We raise our voices in different situations and for different reasons, of which the commonest are: distance, background noise, and a strong emotion. Here are the most usual words for these circumstances:

SHOUT ~ YELL ~ CRY ~ CRY OUT ~ BAWL ~ SCREAM ~ SHRIEK ~ SCREECH ~ SQUEAL
(These are not in alphabetic order)

Shout

This is probably the best known of all these words, as it serves for any of the above cases. However, on account of the different quality of voice, we seldom use this for women or little children: it is *characteristically male*, and the purpose is essentially *to make yourself heard*:

> *You can shout as much as you like, but she won't hear you – she's as deaf as a post.*
>
> *Excited shouts could be heard from the football field.*
>
> *"You wait till I catch you!" shouted the fat man furiously.*

Yell

We **yell** in *an emergency*, when there is no time to think ahead and calculate the volume of voice needed, so a **yell** is likely to be shorter but much wilder than a shout. It expresses *pain, anger, desperation, or excitement*:

> *The harder his father beat him, the louder the boy's yells echoed.*
>
> *"Get back in the car!" yelled Jerry in panic.*
>
> *"Kill them, kill them!" the mob was yelling hysterically.*

Cry

This word is old-fashioned now as a verb of communication, although in the nineteenth century it was used where *nowadays we would say "exclaim"*. You find it in the novels of Jane Austen, for instance. As a noun, it really corresponds to the following verb (**cry out**), being an exclamation of pain or of sudden emotion:

> *There were cries of protest when it was announced that the pop concert was to be cancelled.*

Cry out

This verb is very much used today, as it indicates *fright or sudden pain or indignation*:

> *His wrist must have been sprained in the fall, because he cried out when I touched it.*

Bawl

This is so exceptionally loud that it is often incomprehensible. The reason is that we are so angry that *it doesn't matter whether we are understood or not*: the important thing is to relieve the fury or exasperation we feel:

> *He bawled something furious about calling the police and slammed the door in my face.*

Scream

This is a very high-pitched sound that is alarming to hear because we associate it with *sudden great pain or terror*. In many cases, though, the cause is simply *uncontrolled anger* or – especially with children – *excitement*:

> *Suddenly the lights went out and moments later there came a long scream from the bedroom.*
>
> *As he raced down the path away from the house, he could hear the woman screaming imprecations after him.*
>
> *Our kids scream with delight whenever they see that they're being taken to the funfair.*

Shriek

Similar to **scream** in pitch and likewise caused (mainly) by *terror or despair*, this sound is much *shorter but even wilder*. Whereas even men can scream at moments of extreme suffering, shrieking sounds almost inhuman and is frequently found in tales of *madness or the supernatural*:

> *With a ghastly shriek, she flung herself off the parapet.*

> *Shrieking women fled in panic as the building burst into flames.*

Screech

This is the kind of *long, loud, harsh sound* made by certain birds (owls, parrots, etc.) and also by car-tyres when braking hard, so when applied to a human being it indicates some wild emotion such as fury:

> *All we could hear was the peacocks screeching on the lawn.*

> *The wicked queen let out a screech of rage when her mirror told her that Snow-white was still alive.*

Squeal

Although it is not harsh, this is very like **screech** in pitch and aural penetration. It is usually repeated and often very protracted. We associate it mostly with frightened small animals, and consequently it is often used to describe *children who are frightened or in pain*:

> *The nurse had to struggle to hold the squealing baby still while she tried to sterilise its wounds.*

> *There were frantic squeals from the terrified piglets as the farmer tried to catch them.*

73 MATTER ~ AFFAIR ~ ISSUE ~ PROBLEM ~ SUBJECT ~ THEME ~ TOPIC

Matter

A **matter** is mostly a *circumstance that is important (especially to an individual or to an organization of some sort)*, and in that sense it is therefore also regarded as something personal and private. (Compare this characteristic with **affair, issue** and **topic**):

> *I realized that my nightmares were becoming a matter that needed psychological help.*

> *How and when to approach the professor was a matter of great worry to the young journalist.*

It is necessary to remember that "matters" tend to affect one person (or one group) rather than the general public, unless they are of national importance. If we say "no matter", we usually mean that it doesn't affect us personally. We also refer to "matters of State" to describe things beyond the reach and understanding of the common citizen.

In this connection, the verb **to matter** has a close affinity with the noun, as it means *to be important (to someone)*.

Affair

An **affair** is an *intimate relationship* between two people:

> *Her books, specializing in affairs of the heart, were very popular among women readers.*

But it can also be the kind of relationship that not everyone approves of and is therefore mostly carried on in secret, particularly when it is *sexual, immoral or criminal in character*, so when discovered and made public it becomes a sensation:

> *Everyone in the street knew about Henry's affair with his neighbour's wife – except her husband.*
>
> *The Fowler affair dominated newspaper headlines for weeks.*

However, the plural form (affairs) is regularly used for perfectly respectable *dealings between nations*:

> *The Foreign Affairs Secretary is to fly to Moscow next week to discuss the matter with the Russians.*

Issue

When an idea becomes *highly polemic*, arousing strong feelings and dividing people into opposed groups, we call it "an issue":

> *In some societies, abortion is simply a matter of personal choice, but in others it is regarded as an issue of maximum importance.*

To "make an issue" of something means to treat what others consider trivial as a very serious matter, usually as a pretext for a quarrel:

> *James had never worried about his little dog's barking until the people next door made an issue of it, threatening to call the police unless he did something about it.*

Problem

We can't use this word for just any negative situation; a problem in English is something that troubles us but that we know *has a solution* (if we can find it) and the situation won't improve until we apply that solution:

> *Acne is a problem that affects many young people, but it usually disappears by itself after a few years.*

If we say that "someone is a problem", we mean that that person is causing us unnecessary trouble. (For **trouble**, see separate entry.)

Subject

This word has two basic meanings:

1. As *a person* it means one who belongs to a particular nation and has to abide by its laws:

    > *A British passport is not available to immigrants unless they are declared British subjects.*

2. As *a thing* it is something we talk about, think about, dream about, write or read about, or something (or someone) chosen to draw, paint, examine, or study (especially at school):

    > *Love is the preferred subject of countless songs and poems.*
    >
    > *I'm afraid teenage sex isn't the kind of subject our group would readily choose for discussion.*
    >
    > *For the subjects of this research we selected twenty confirmed and long-term smokers.*

Theme

We use this word for subjects of *artistic (especially musical) works or formal academic study*:

> *Wagner employed the term "Leitmotif" for the theme he used to introduce or describe a distinctive character or situation in his operas.*
>
> *The theme of our discussion that day was "The status symbol in late Twentieth-Century life".*

Topic

A topic is nothing more than the subject people choose *for conversation* when they meet. It may sometimes be important, but it is more likely to be trivial in character and neutral in tone, so that everyone may join in without fear of offending or antagonizing the others:

> *If people in England find themselves forced to make conversation with complete strangers, they take refuge in the safest topic, which is always the weather.*

74 MISCHIEVOUS ~ MALICIOUS ~ SPITEFUL ~ VICIOUS

Mischievous

This is not normally a strong word. It generally shows a playful desire to cause *temporary trouble for others*, as is typical in children, who don't realize how serious their action may be. But occasionally, in grown-ups, it means a more reprehensible kind of behaviour, where the trouble planned is quite serious:

> *She is a mischievous child, always ready to play pranks to discomfort other children.*

Malicious

Here is a word we use for adults who know the harm they are trying to cause – and probably enjoy it. It indicates a *desire to hurt, even when the consequences are recognized*:

> *From the malicious look he gave me, it was clear he was waiting to hit me the moment I turned my back.*

Spiteful

Again more characteristic of children, this behaviour shows a *wish to hurt* – physically if possible, and merely for the sake of hurting, but again without considering the consequences:

> *He has the spiteful habit of suddenly pulling the hair of the little girl who sits in front of him and laughing when she yells.*

Vicious

In the sense of causing damage, it shows a stronger form of **spite**, where *the urge to hurt overrides other feelings*:

> *One of the attackers turned back as they were going and gave their prostrate victim a vicious kick in the stomach.*

75 NORTH ~ NORTHERN ~ NORTHERLY

While **north** can be a noun (the name of one of the four cardinal directions), all the above are also adjectives, and there are the following differences between them:

North

In weather matters, this tells us the *origin* of a wind (the cardinal point from which it blows):

> *In the Southern Hemisphere, it is the south wind that brings the cold weather.*

It often forms *part of the name* of any town or territory of which there is a second part, with exactly the same name, in the opposite direction – in this case the south. The distinction may be administrative or political.

> Examples: *North Dakota, North Carolina, North Korea and North Yemen.*

Northern

It is a geographic word, referring to that part of a town or land *situated to the north* of the central area. (See the above example for **north**). It is a very general term and there is no way of identifying any boundary. Northern Italy would certainly include the Po valley, but it is a matter for the individual whether to include, say, Florence in that area or not. Similarly, northern Chile is the part of that country that is closest to Peru; and in the USA the Americans distinguish clearly between northern and southern California – two recognized divisions of a single state, and in this case with a clear territorial boundary.

Northerly

It is used for *direction of movement*, so a northerly current in the sea would be one flowing more or less towards the north, while a northerly route would be a route leading to the north.

N.B. All the above forms and comments are similarly valid for the other cardinal points: *south, east* and *west*.

76 OBVIOUS ~ EVIDENT ~ APPARENT ~ PATENT ~ BLATANT

All these adjectives refer to the impression we get when we look at something (or when we hear it or sense it in some other way), but the differences between them are a matter of *what we think about that impression*.

Obvious

This means that *we are convinced by what we see*; there is no doubt because everything about it is clear to us:

> *The dog showed obvious anger.*

> *It was obvious that the dog was angry.*
> It was snarling or growling, which are unmistakable signs of anger in a dog

Evident

Here we can see enough to suggest a good explanation, but *the facts we see don't fully convince us* that our supposition is absolutely right:

> *The owners of the house had left in evident panic, for there was a half-eaten meal on the table and one of the chairs had been overturned.*
> The added information shows that the observer is still trying to satisfy himself as to the cause of the mess.

Apparent

What we see in this case doesn't convince us, because *the evidence is insufficient or could offer several explanations*, but we have nothing more definite to conclude from:

> *It is apparent that the house is empty. No-one has been seen entering or leaving it and the windows are never opened.*
> This doesn't mean that the house is in reality empty: it may be occupied by a recluse, or the occupants may come and go under cover of darkness.

Patent

A rather literary alternative to **obvious**:

> *Her relief at getting a seat was patent, as though she had been standing too long and her legs were aching.*

Blatant

This adjective, which is very much used with abstract nouns, is strongly negative and means three things: that what is shown is unquestionably clear; that the observer disapproves of it; and that the person who is doing it or has done it is *making no effort to hide the fact*:

> *He was driving with blatant disregard of the law – fast and recklessly, obliging other drivers to avoid him at all costs.*

> *His words were a blatant insult, as if he wanted to provoke a violent reaction.*

N.B. **Blatant** cannot (unlike the others in this group) be used in the structure "It is/was... that... ".

77 OCCASION ~ OPPORTUNITY ~ CHANCE

Occasion

An **occasion** is one of the following:

1. The moment, or the date, when *a certain action takes place*:

   > The witness stated that on the occasion in question he had been out of the country.
   > As this is in a court of law, the occasion is obviously one when a crime was committed.

2. The time chosen for *a ceremony*:

   > This hall is hired out for weddings, christenings, parties and similar occasions.
   >
   > His retirement party was an occasion none of us will ever forget!

3. The moment we consider most favourable for *doing something important, and perhaps risky*:

   > I always hated writing, so I used to wait for a suitable occasion such as a birthday when I had to send a letter.

Opportunity

An **opportunity** is a good or appropriate moment for doing something *we have been wanting to do*:

> They took the first opportunity to go and see him after his operation.
>
> The lecturer paused to glance at his notes, and Sheila seized this opportunity to ask him her question.

Chance

This can describe luck or the fortuitous development of events, as in "by chance", but in the following cases, **chance** is sometimes confused with **occasion.**

1. One meaning is *a moment to act*. It may not be the best moment, but what we have to do is *so important or so urgent* that we have to act now, before the action becomes impossible:

The guard stopped to light a cigarette, and this momentary distraction was the chance the prisoners had been hoping for to make their escape.

They arrived so shortly before departure that they had no chance of changing their currency.

N.B.   In both these examples, **opportunity** could be used, but it is less dramatic than **chance**.

2.   Or it can mean *a possibility or possibilities of success* in something we are going to do:

What are my chances if I send them an application?

I know she's only a beginner, but I think she deserves a chance.

78 PAY ~ PAY FOR

Pay without **for**

1.   Being transitive, **to pay** takes two objects, a *direct object* (the thing that is paid – usually some form of money), and an *indirect object* (the person who receives what is paid), but it is possible to omit one or other, or even both, when the nature of what is paid or the person who receives the money is clear from the situation.

Thus, when we take a taxi, we can *pay the driver* or *pay the fare*, but it would be unnecessary to say: *Pay the driver the fare*, because the driver is the only person we would pay and the fare is the only thing we have to pay:

There's the rent to pay at the end of this month!

There's no hurry: you can pay me back whenever you like.

2.   If it *is* necessary to include both objects, we put the indirect one first, as with other verbs, like *tell* and *ask*, unless the indirect object is an exceptional one or is unusually long, when "to" is needed:

Most tourists pay their guide what he asks without question.

She was inclined to pay the fee to anyone who looked official, which was very foolish.

3.   The *people* we pay are generally those who have earned the money, but *what* we can pay is far more varied: bills, fees, wages, prices, charges, costs, fines, taxes, rent, etc. – and certain spoken things that *don't* represent money, for example a *tribute* or a *compliment*:

> *We've got seven bills to pay this month!*
>
> *Is your salary paid, like mine, direct into the bank?*
>
> *Nobody bothers to pay parking fines – until their car is towed away!*
>
> *The speaker paid a glowing tribute to the work done by his predecessor.*

Pay for

For is necessary *only when we state the cause of the payment*. For instance, we pay a shopkeeper *for* the article we are buying, or we pay a workman *for* the work he has done:

> *I paid five hundred dollars for that picture over there.*
>
> *You have to pay the technician for just coming to the house, even if he doesn't have to make any repairs!*
>
> *Do we pay anything in the museum for children, do you know?*
>
> *Whom should I pay for looking after my car?*

N.B.   Don't forget that in *passive* sentences, **for** must not be omitted:

> Shop notice*: Broken articles must be paid for.*
>
> *I've just realized that the wedding photos have still to be paid for.*

79 PLAGUE ~ PEST ~ BLIGHT

Plague

This is either:

1.   A *severe epidemic deriving from a disease spread by (animal) bearers*, such as the plagues that coincided with the appearance in medieval Europe of new species of rats:

> *The plague known as the Black Death killed millions of Europeans in the Middle Ages.*

or:

2. Some kind of widespread infestation, usually in the form of *a large number of insects or similar small animals*, concentrated in one area, that attack us or our livestock or crops:

    Africa is prone to recurrent plagues of locusts.

Pest

Nowadays this refers to *any animal that is exceptionally destructive* to man or the plants he is cultivating, either because of its habits or because of its large numbers. This means that even relatively harmless animals can become pests if their habitual food supply has been reduced (as with foxes) or, in the absence of natural enemies, they have been able to multiply excessively (as with rabbits in Australia):

    Mink, foolishly released from captivity, and in large numbers, have quickly become a threat to so many forms of wildlife that they are classified as a dangerous pest.

Blight

This is the term for certain *afflictions of plants*, caused by microscopic fungus or by minute creatures that attack and destroy different parts of a plant. Obviously the kind of blight that most concerns us is one that damages crops:

    One of the worst blights to which orange trees are susceptible is the so-called mildew.

80 PLENTY ~ FULL

Let's begin with **Full,** as it is easy to explain.

Full

This is a well-known adjective, with the meaning that *no more can be added* to the space in question:

    Bobby, don't talk with your mouth full!

    By the time they arrived the restaurant was full and they had to wait an hour for a table.

At this time of day the buses are full of commuters on their way home.

Plenty

This is a noun, not an adjective. It means *more (of something) than is needed*, so it is incorrect to say: *The room was plenty of people.* You have to say: *The room was full of people.*

To use **plenty** correctly, it is advisable to use a verb like "there is" or "to have":

> *There were plenty of vacant tables in the restaurant, so we had no difficulty in finding one with a view of the lake.*

> *My train wasn't leaving for another hour, so I had plenty of time to look for a good book to read on the journey.*

> *Please don't hesitate to take another sandwich if you fancy one; I've got plenty more in the kitchen.*

(Also see **Full, Sheer, Utter**)

81 POLITE ~ COURTEOUS ~ CIVIL

These are the adjectives for the respective concepts of *politeness, courtesy* and *civility*, which all refer to ways of speaking or ways of behaving towards others in social contexts.

Polite

When we refer to **polite** in *speech*, we mean that someone:

- uses the correct title or name in addressing another person;
- employs the kind of language the other will understand;
- avoids unkind or coarse expressions.

When it is a matter of *behaviour*, that person:

- behaves in a way that cannot offend;
- modifies his manner if it is evidently unsuitable;

- shows respect for the other;
- listens attentively when someone else is speaking;
- does not interrupt or change the subject abruptly;
- allows the other person time to comprehend and think;
- responds appropriately to changes of situation.

Courteous

Courtesy is more than **politeness**, because it includes all the above factors, but in a clearly kind and helpful way, *showing consideration for the other person's physical and mental comfort*. In some situations courtesy involves doing things that are not even expected, purely for the other person's sake, such as:

- giving that person prior attention;
- dissimulating boredom;
- anticipating the other's needs;
- repeating information that was evidently not well understood;
- raising or lowering the voice when desirable;
- giving up a seat or providing a chair;
- helping someone to sit down or get up;
- showing sympathy for the other's emotional state.

Civil

Civility in personal relationships means using all the expected forms of behaviour, but *without sincerity or personal interest*, although avoiding open rudeness.

82 PORT ~ HARBOUR ~ HAVEN

Harbour (US harbor)

We use this for a coastal formation that, because of its position and shape (usually a curve, often with hills round it) *affords protection for shipping* from storms, high winds, and rough seas:

> *Being experienced sailors, the Phoenicians always chose natural, enclosed (and defensible) harbours like Cartagena, where their vessels were safe from storms and enemies alike.*

Port

Here we think of a place, either on a coast or on a river, that is *suitable for vessels to load and unload.* That is, it contains quays and cranes, and mostly provides complete docking facilities. All this also requires associated buildings such as offices and warehouses, and in many cases customs offices; consequently ports usually develop into waterside towns:

> *When a big ship comes into the port, our town is soon full of sailors out for a good time.*

> *Shipping companies that wish to use these docks have to make prior arrangements with the port authorities.*

Ports are not necessarily natural harbours, and often the reason for their existence is the presence of a nearby inland town that needs access to the water, as in the case of Athens and Piraeus.

Haven

These days this word, which once meant the same as **harbour**, is purely figurative and poetic, referring to some (often imaginary) place where certain kinds of people can live without fear:

> *These islands have become a haven for international criminal organizations, which know they are safe from the police here.*

83 POSTURE

Apart from the straightforward standing, sitting, kneeling, and lying, there are many other postures we, and other animals, can adopt. Here are the most common verbs for these movements, in alphabetic order:

**BUNCH ~ CROUCH ~ HUDDLE ~ LEAN ~
LOLL ~ SPRAWL ~ SQUAT ~ STOOP**

Bunch (also noun)

This is a group action: animals such as fishes, birds, or sheep *that feel in danger* press themselves together to present the appearance of being a mass, which daunts a potential attacker:

> *These caterpillars bunch when moving as a protection against predatory birds.*

Crouch

To bend the knees, bringing the body *close to the ground*. In humans, it is a method of relaxing from the standing position or a way of getting close to something of interest on the ground. In many animals, it is a means of hiding or a preparation for attacking:

> *Our Indian guide suddenly stopped and crouched over some marks beside the path we were following.*

> *I could see something dark, possibly a leopard, crouching behind the bushes.*

Huddle (also noun)

Again, a group action: each person or animal *presses itself tightly against the rest*, either to feel safer or because it is cold:

> *The lost children were found eventually, huddling under some steps, too afraid to move.*

Lean

To incline the body *away from the strictly vertical position*, for various reasons: to rest the body, to bring the head closer to something or to keep it away, and in many cases simply to show more or less interest:

On finishing his writing, he leaned back in his chair and stretched luxuriously.

Loll

To stretch out in a chair, or at full length on a bed, in an attitude that shows *no interest in any activity*:

> *When we went in, we found him lolling in an armchair, gazing at the ceiling, instead of working.*

Sprawl

A stage further than **lolling**, in which the *arms and legs are fully extended*, taking up a lot of room – usually to the annoyance of other people:

> *George was sprawling on the sofa, obliging everyone to step over his legs as they came in.*

Squat

To sit with your *legs crossed*. It is a customary way of sitting in many societies; but when a chair would have been more normal, this posture often suggests that the squatter does not intend to move, which is why this verb is so much used nowadays to describe the (illegal) occupation of an empty building:

> *The tribesmen were all squatting round a fire, where a lamb was being roasted whole.*
>
> *The children came and squatted beside him to see what he had drawn on the pavement.*

Stoop (also noun)

The body bends *forward at the level of the shoulders*. This is often done to see better from the standing position, but in some cases (very tall people who are over-conscious of their height, for instance) it has become permanent:

> *I found I had been stooping over the cooking-pot for several minutes and now my back was aching.*
>
> *He was so tall that he had to stoop every time he entered a room.*
>
> *This stoop had become habitual in him.*

84 PREOCCUPY ~ WORRY

Preoccupy

This verb has a quite literal meaning: *occupy before* (the present moment or the present object). When it refers to the mind (and the verb is almost always used passively then), the meaning is that the mind is already occupied with some other thought or activity; that is, that the person is busy thinking something already when a new situation develops and he cannot suddenly leave that earlier thought in order to start thinking about the new, changed circumstances:

> *I was too preoccupied with bringing my address-book up to date to notice how dark the room had become.*

Worry

This, when used intransitively, means to *allow anxiety to dominate one's mind*; a problem keeps coming into one's mind, to the exclusion of other thoughts, distressing the thinker and preventing him from considering the matter rationally:

> *She found herself worrying stupidly again about the effect of her comments on her husband's family, although common sense told her that she had said nothing untoward.*

85 PRESERVE ~ CONSERVE

These two verbs are so similar that we very easily confuse them, perhaps not even realizing there is any difference.

Preserve

The meaning is *keep something unchanged*, and this is achieved by taking steps to prevent any alteration in size, substance, shape, content, colour, or whatever other aspect is important:

> *The ancient Egyptians preserved their dead by mummifying them.*

Fresh fruit is preserved for future consumption in the form of jam or marmalade – known collectively as "preserves".

Interesting dead animals are preserved – at least outwardly – by taxidermy.

The fresh condition of food is preserved for a time by storing it in a refrigerator.

Conserve

This means *use so sparingly that there will always be enough left* – a very different sense from **preserve**. In other words, when something is in short supply and there is a danger of exhausting that quantity, we continue to use it (we have no choice!) but we restrict its consumption to ensure that we shall not be left without any. This is important for limited supplies of any sort, such as food, medicines, or energy, and is especially relevant today in the matter of ecology:

A person stranded in the desert should make every effort to conserve his water supply by frugal drinking, and his strength by taking shelter during the heat of the day and doing his walking at night.

The authorities try to conserve water by exhorting the public not to use it too liberally at any time, and to economize severely in times of drought.

We endeavour to conserve those plant and animal species that are described as "endangered" by stopping their destruction or the destruction of their habitats.

86 PRIVATE ~ INTIMATE ~ INTIMACY ~ TO INTIMATE ~ INTIMATION

Private

The basic meaning is *not for general knowledge or use*. In other words, it refers to *what concerns an individual or a restricted group only* and is the opposite of **public**, which is for the use or knowledge of everybody:

This club is private; we do not admit non-members.

My medical society ensures that I always get a private room in hospital.

Intimate (adjective) and **Intimacy** (noun)

The adjective has the meaning of *private between two*, as its essential idea is that of a shared relationship that is barred to outsiders. An **intimate** friend is one who is allowed into our deepest secrets. The noun **intimacy** describes a relationship in which nothing is hidden between the partners, and is very often sexual in nature:

> *That is something I would confess to only the most intimate of friends.*

> *She was too ill to protest when the nurses undressed her and did things that offended her sense of intimacy.*

Intimate (verb)
This verb, however, has nothing to do with **intimacy** in modern English; it means *to give some indication without specific details:*

> *My boss has intimated that I might expect promotion, but I do wish he would be more explicit: how much? When? - Those are the questions that interest me!*

Intimation
This is the noun corresponding to the verb above. Its meaning is like *suggestion, hint* or *warning:*

> *They greeted us in their usual friendly way, so we had absolutely no intimation that they had taken offence and were intending to sue us.*

(Also see **Hint, Imply, Intimate, Insinuate**)

87 PRODUCT ~ PRODUCE

Product (countable)

A **product** is something *made or manufactured*, or an item of food or drink that has *been changed* from its original, natural form, often by processing it.

Examples of products are: clothing, furniture, refrigerators, sausages (originally meat), and wine (originally grape juice).

Produce (uncountable)

It is the original article of food or drink, perhaps washed or treated to preserve its qualities, and certainly prepared for transport and sale, but otherwise *presented in its natural and recognizable form.*

Examples are: honey, fruit, fresh fish, and milk (always pasteurized to make it safe for immediate consumption or sterilized to make it last longer).

88 PULLING

When you want to express the idea of pulling, consider how much additional information you can provide by choosing one of the following, which not only tell us how the pulling is done but reveal the circumstances.

(Ways of Pulling)

DRAG ~ DRAW ~ HAUL ~ HOIST ~ LUG ~ TOW ~ TRAIL ~ TUG

Drag

The object (a carpet, furniture, ...) is *too heavy to be lifted*, so the pulling is done along the ground:

> *The murderer then took hold of his victim by the feet and dragged the body into the next room, where it was found later that day.*

Draw

Probably the oldest of all these verbs, this means "pull", but in a *multiplicity of situations* (especially in its many phrasal forms), as the following examples will show you:

> *I suppose we call it drawing because we have to pull the pencil across the paper to make a picture.*
>
> *A draught horse is an exceptionally strong animal used for drawing heavy carts.*
>
> *The crowd drew back in alarm when the strange object rose into the air.*
>
> *His lungs wheezed appallingly every time he drew a breath.*

He drew his sword and cut the giant knot in two.

You must have drawn the wrong conclusion, you know.

This chimney has never drawn well: it tends to fill the room with smoke.

Haul

This is really a manner of transporting (the noun is "haulage") in which a heavy or bulky object is moved (probably by **towing** it – see below) *over a long distance*:

> *We suppose that the massive stones used in building these pyramids were hauled to the site on rollers and then pushed or pulled into position by slaves.*

Hoist

A form of *lifting*: the object is raised by a rope that passes over a pulley:

> *In the old days furniture that could not be carried up the stairs had to be hoisted up the outside of the building.*

Lug

To *half carry* something too heavy or cumbersome to be raised off the ground. It is from this verb that we have the noun "luggage":

> *I've been lugging this Christmas tree from room to room for the past hour, and Mother still can't decide where to stand it.*

Tow

This, deriving from an old word for "rope", means *using a rope or chain to pull something* that, being on wheels or in water, will move, but only with some effort:

> *Our car stopped altogether fives miles outside Dijon, and we had to call a breakdown van to tow us into the town.*

Trail

To *pull behind you*. This is used when the object is too long, or you are too tired to carry it:

> *The road was lined with exhausted refugees, trailing their belongings in the dust.*

Tug

To pull *quickly or sharply*, either because you expect to move the object easily or (when it is clothing) because you want attention:

> *The little girl tugged insistently at my sleeve, and I realized that she had something to show me.*

89 PUSHING

If **pushing** means *making something move away*, then these verbs indicate different methods and circumstances. Don't forget that many of these can be used for cases of figurative pushing too.

(Ways of Pushing)

BOOST ~ DRIVE ~ GOAD ~ HEAVE ~ HUSTLE ~ IMPEL ~ JOG ~ JOSTLE ~ LAUNCH ~ NUDGE ~ POKE ~ PRESS ~ PROD ~ PROPEL ~ SHOVE ~ STUB ~ THRUST

Boost

We add *sudden extra force* to the push to increase the momentum. In rocket propulsion, a **booster** is a second container of powerful fuel that gives the rocket the additional force needed to escape the Earth's gravity:

> *The arrival of reinforcements greatly boosted the defenders' morale and encouraged them to hold out longer.*

Drive

This verb combines two notions: that of *force* and that of *planned direction*, which is why it is so much used with vehicles:

> *The dogs helped him to drive the sheep into their fold.*
>
> *I had to use a very heavy hammer to drive the nails into such hard wood.*
>
> *That noise is driving me mad!*

Goad

A goad is a pointed instrument that hurts when pushed into the body, so this word as a verb means to **drive** by *using pain* (physical or mental):

It was his wife's tantrums that goaded him into seeking divorce.

Such sustained oppression eventually goaded the longsuffering populace to action.

Heave

The object you want to move is very heavy indeed and needs *a great (often concerted) effort*:

Summoning all their strength, the men heaved together and the boat slid slowly across the sand and into the water.

Hustle

To push someone along *very hastily*, as in an emergency, when there is no time to waste:

Seeing that the minister was in physical danger from the crowd, his bodyguards hustled him into his car and drove off.

Impel

This verb is most used in technical descriptions of movement, but it often serves for an *inner feeling of compulsion* to take some action:

Her indignation impelled her to lodge a complaint about the service.

Jog

Familiar as a gentle way of running, this verb really means *giving a slight push*, or several slight pushes:

Another customer jogged his arm in passing and made him drop his glasses.

Please jog my memory, will you: I know you're Harry's son, but I just can't recall your name.

Jostle

Usually a crowd of people is needed for this, as the action is one of pushing a person in *different directions at almost the same moment*, which can be rather violent:

We were jostled so roughly by the crowd leaving the stadium that I lost one of my shoes.

Launch

To start a *movement that will thereafter continue*, probably at a constant speed. You can use it for an object like a rocket, or for yourself – in the sense of beginning a long action:

The ship was duly launched yesterday, by the mayoress, and of course with a bottle of champagne.

It was my grandfather who launched me into business.

After some hesitation, he launched into an impassioned speech about saving the whales.

Nudge

To give someone a *small push with one elbow* in order to prompt or remind him to do something:

As soon as you nudged me, I remembered what I had forgotten to ask.

Poke

To *push a long, pointed object* (a stick, a finger, etc.) into something, generally with certain care. There are various reasons for this: to test its consistency, to see whether it is alive, to find out how it will react, etc.:

The old gentleman peered closely at the object on the pavement and then poked it cautiously with his umbrella.

Press

To *push steadily* in order to extract a liquid or leave a mark; to push yourself forward in the effort to reach a certain position; or to push something like a button with one finger:

The juice obtained by pressing grapes is called must.

Her fans pressed excitedly round her.

Please press the bell for service.

Prod

This is very similar to **poke** and is done for similar reasons, but not gently and *we repeat the action* until something happens:

> *The dog lay still on the pavement, but when Madeline prodded it with her foot it jumped up and ran away.*

> *The old fellow refused to speak, even with his wife prodding him in the back.*

Propel

Like **drive**, this indicates *steady pushing in a certain direction*, especially when a mechanical **propeller** is used:

> *It is the continuous expulsion of these gases that propels the rocket into the atmosphere.*

Shove

To push once, *suddenly and violently*:

> *The moment he opened the door, the footman was shoved roughly aside and the mob streamed in.*

Stub

Either to *hit your toe* violently against a small, unnoticed obstacle, or (with "out") to *press a cigarette* against a hard surface in order to extinguish it:

> *He stubbed his left foot against the doorstep and limped painfully into the room.*

> *Please stub all cigarettes out before entering the hall.*

Thrust

To push something hard and quickly. There is often a *sense of emergency*:

> *The mother managed to thrust her baby under the table seconds before the house collapsed on them.*

> *As the fugitive ran past her he thrust something small and hard into her hand.*

90 QUICK ~ FAST ~ RAPID ~ SWIFT

Quick

This refers to *speed of happening*, so we use it for anything that *happens (or changes or develops)* in a short time, perhaps almost at once:

> *A quick answer, a quick trip, quick growth.*

Fast

This describes *the great rate of progress and travel* at which an object is moving or of which it is capable:

> *A fast current, fast thinking, a fast car.*

(Remember that **fast** is also an adverb, with the same meaning).

Rapid

This is an alternative to **fast**, but either:

- there is a strong sense of *constant movement* but with less speed:

  > *A rapid stream, rapid speech.*

- or the action is *repeated at very short intervals*:

  > *Rapid eye movements, rapid changes of direction.*

Swift

Like **fast**, this word describes great speed, but it also stresses that *the movement is easy*, without any kind of friction or obstacle, and that the trajectory is a more or less straight line. Those noisy dark birds, with curved wings like those of swallows, that we find flying high over our towns in summer are called "swifts" because of their speed:

> *The swift passage of comets through space.*

91 RATHER THAN

When followed by a verb, this prepositional phrase changes meaning according to whether the following verb is a gerund or an infinitive (a "zero infinitive" – without the "to" particle).

1. If the following verb is a gerund, **rather than** has the same meaning as *instead of*, although it is less explicit:

    Rather than serving his country, he could be described as exploiting it.
    Here, the man is assumed to be serving his country (in one of the national forces, perhaps, or in a political role) but in reality he is using his position to benefit himself. So we could also say "Instead of serving his country..."

Note that a gerund is not the only word that can follow **rather than**; with the same function it can also be followed by a noun, an adjective, or an adverb:

> *Rather than a house in the country, I would choose a flat in town now.*
>
> *Rather than simply fat, the woman was spherical in shape.*
>
> *I had warned her to be careful in opening the parcel, but rather than carefully, she was doing it absolutely gingerly, as if she thought it might bite her.*

2. If the following verb is a zero infinitive, **rather than** tells us that the action it describes is something the doer decides against, whereas the action that *he opts for* is expressed in the other verb, as here:

    Rather than wait for a taxi that might never appear, I set off to walk the two miles to the station.

    Their spokesman stated that the workers were prepared to take a pay cut rather than lose their jobs altogether.

Note that with the infinitive construction, the other verb in the sentence may be expressed in any tense or mood:

> *Rather than be thought mean, he insisted/insists/will insist, etc. on paying the restaurant bill when dining out in company.*

92 REACH ~ ATTAIN ~ ACHIEVE ~ OBTAIN

Reach

Basically, there are two meanings:

1. *To extend part of the body* towards something. This is most often an arm and hand, but it could equally be a leg or the head, or even part of the face, such as the nose, chin, or tongue. Effort is needed, but if by doing this you touch the object, then you have **reached** it:

   She was so small that even by standing on tiptoe, she could not quite reach the door handle.

   Chameleons have tongues long enough to reach an insect many centimetres away.

2. *To go in a certain direction* as far as the objective. When there is physical movement, the verb has the same meaning as *arrive at* or *extend to*. But immobile things that are by their nature long, like roads or cables, can also be said to **reach** a determined point, although there is no movement:

   The expedition reached its destination a week early.

   Many African rivers dry up before they can reach the sea.

   The snowflakes melted as they reached the ground.

   The border between the two countries reaches the ocean.

   Her hair was so long that it reached her waist.

   Our municipal transport system reaches all districts of the city.

Attain

This is the same as **reach**, but in a more *abstract sense*, and what is reached is arrived at without effort, as part of the natural development of affairs, such as different ages:

   In Europe we attain our majority at the age of eighteen.

Achieve

This is like saying *reach and keep*, that is, *the effort made is to possess the thing*, and that thing is something non-material, such as *an objective, a purpose, or an ambition*:

> *By marrying into the aristocracy, he achieved his aim of becoming rich and famous.*

Obtain

This is a more abstract form of "get". Effort is again required and *the thing desired becomes a possession*, but, unlike verbs such as buy, steal, or capture, it doesn't tell us *how* the thing has become a possession:

> *He somehow obtained a permit to sell in the street market.*

> *"Where did you obtain this?" asked the police inspector, staring deep into my eyes.*

93 REALIZE ~ NOTICE

While both of these mean that we become suddenly aware of a fact or circumstance, the difference is in the part of our body involved.

Let's begin with **notice**:

Notice

We notice *with our sense organs* (eyes, ears, nose, skin,...); that is, we see or hear or smell or feel or taste something:

> *As we approached the cottage, we both noticed that the new owners had done quite a lot to brighten it and make it more welcoming. The windows had been repainted and the garden was now full of flowering plants.*

> *The man was obviously born locally, but I noticed that the woman spoke with an unfamiliar accent.*

> *Nobody noticed the smell of burning coming from the kitchen until the smoke alarm suddenly sounded.*

> *My mother hates the taste of garlic and she always notices when there's garlic in a dish.*

Realize

But we realize *with our brain*: our senses have failed to inform us and it is in our head that the awareness (usually that a change has taken place) appears:

> *It was when I suddenly shivered that I realized that the fire, which was behind me, had gone out while I was studying.*

> *He was confident that his Greek was good, but this woman looked so shocked when he spoke that he realized he must have said something awful by mistake.*

> *But didn't you realize you were on the wrong bus when it turned off the High Street instead of carrying on to the station?*

94 RELATION ~ RELATIONS ~ RELATIONSHIP

Relation

A **relation** can mean *an account of something that has happened*, or *a person of the same family* (that is, a relative), but more usually it refers to *the connection we make in our mind between one thing and another*:

> *Is there any relation between these changes in the weather and global warming, I wonder?*

Relations

It refers to the constantly changing degree of friendliness – or hostility – between two people or two nations and to the extent to which they are prepared to maintain contact:

> *The appointment of this new ambassador has led to a great improvement in relations between our two countries.*

Relationship

This is the particular *connection that exists* between any two people or groups of people, making each one a kind of counterpart of the other. Such a connection may be a matter of family, in which case it is the same as **relation**, or of some developed contact between the two, but most **relationships** are a question of chance. Examples of common relationships are: male – female; husband – wife; parent – child; seller – buyer; neighbours; workmates:

What is the relationship between those two people: are they married, or relatives, or just good friends – or what... ?

Renting a house creates a new relationship in your life: that of tenant to landlord, which isn't always an easy one.

95 RENT ~ HIRE ~ LEASE ~ CHARTER

Certain differences in the use of these words across the Atlantic Ocean have led to confusion of meanings. All of them refer to short-term employment of a person or agreed use of an object belonging to someone else for a stipulated period of time, and for a stipulated payment; but the verb used in the UK differs from the US verb according to the nature of the object used and the conditions of payment:

Hire

1. In Britain, whether a verb or a noun, this is used for the following:

    *   *people* such as interpreters, travel guides, or baby-sitters;

    *   *movable objects* such as television sets, equipment, or vehicles (London taxis bear the sign "For Hire" when unoccupied);

    *   and *places of public use*, such as rooms and halls, but for very short periods, usually no longer than 24 hours.

2. The essential characteristic in all forms of hiring is that the amount charged is *calculated per unit of time (small units: minutes, hours, or days)*:

    We're planning to hire a safari guide as soon as we get to Nairobi.

    Boats for hire. All or half day.

    He called a car-hire firm and arranged for delivery of a Mercedes that same afternoon.

3. In the USA, **hire** is used fundamentally in the sense of "engage" (to employ as a worker):

    The hiring and firing of labour is much simpler in the USA than in the EU.

Rent

As **hire** is associated with employment in America, **rent** tends to be used there for situations that would require **hire** in the UK. This is how the phrase "Rent-a-car" became internationally established.

Conversely, in Britain, **rent** is the verb reserved for the use of property (land or buildings), for which *the charge is calculated on a long-term, yearly basis, which may be divided into smaller periods – weeks or months*:

> *An artistic couple have just rented the cottage for the next six months.*

Lease

This can be considered an extension of **renting**, with the feature that it involves *large areas of land, or national territories* and the periods of time frequently cover many years, as when China leased Hong Kong to Great Britain:

> *The house stands on land leased from the Duchy of Cornwall at the end of the last century.*

Charter

The main use of this verb is with vehicles of public transport when taken for *special purposes or exceptional journeys*:

> *As with aircraft, buses can be chartered for certain trips.*

96 ROAD ~ ROADWAY ~ STREET

The simple difference is that "roads" cross the country and "streets" cross towns, but there are some complications. Let's begin with **street**.

Street

This word is a corruption of the Latin "via strata". At one time all "streets" in Britain had been laid by the Romans, but now the word is limited to city thoroughfares. Even so, the most important of the modern "streets" follow Roman routes. However, certain highways usually radiating out from London (the Roman capital city) are still called "... Street", such as "Watling Street", and some of these can still be traced for miles across England.

Road

This word derives from "to ride", because it referred originally to the kind of track across the country that was followed by horseriders. Nowadays it is used for any made route that links towns, but if we see it as part of the name of a city street, as in The Edgware Road in London, this is because it was once the road that led to Edgware.

Roadway

This term distinguishes the part of any street reserved for the traffic and therefore banned to pedestrians, who are restricted to the "pavements" ("sidewalks" in the USA).

97 ROB ~ STEAL

While these two verbs both mean *the unlawful taking of another person's possession* (and here the victim of this action may be a person or the special building that houses some object of value), there are certain differences to bear in mind.

Differences of circumstance

In the case of a human victim, **robbing** is done openly, usually in his presence, and the robber very often uses violence or the threat of violence to induce the victim to hand over his possessions:

> *Theseus cleared the Isthmus of the many bandits who used to rob, and often kill, innocent travellers.*

When the **robbing** takes place in a quiet building (a museum, a church, etc.) it is usually done when the building is empty, because this gives the robbers time to commit the crime efficiently, but banks are often robbed in broad daylight, and then the customers find themselves involved too:

A robber who knew what to look for broke into this Basilica last month, and took all the silver items on the altar and in those glass cases.

Were you in the bank yesterday when those robbers burst in and a security guard was injured in the shooting?

Stealing is done in secret, either when the victim is absent or while he is unable to realize what is happening:

Burglars got into our house last year and stole all my husband's trophies.

Somebody stole the purse out of my mother's bag while she was at the market the other day.

Differences of grammar

When the stolen object is mentioned the verb **to rob** needs the preposition "of":

Highwaymen used to hold coaches up on this moor and rob the passengers of everything of value.

When the place where the object was kept is mentioned the verb **to steal** takes "from":

Somebody stole our football tickets from my pocket only minutes after I had bought them!

In the passive voice, it is *the victim* who (or which, for places) **is robbed** but *the object of value* that **is stolen**:

My aunt's taxi was stopped on the way to the hotel and she was robbed at gunpoint of all her money.

Our local museum has been robbed three times this year.

Put those bank notes in a safe or at least out of sight, otherwise they'll be stolen in no time!

98 RUNNING ~ JUMPING

As with **walking**, there are many verbs that, especially for animals, indicate different manners of fast movement. Here are some of the more important ones.

BELT ~ BOLT ~ BOUND ~ BUCK ~ CANTER ~ DART ~ DASH ~ FRISK ~ GALLOP ~ GAMBOL ~ HOP ~ LEAP ~ LOPE ~ POP ~ POUNCE ~ RACE ~ SCAMPER ~ SCRAMBLE ~ SCUTTLE ~ SHOOT ~ SKIP ~ SPRING ~ VAULT

Belt

A slang word for very fast running.

Bolt

To run wildly, in fear or panic, usually to escape some real or imagined danger. Horses are notorious for doing this.

Bound

This is a form of repeated jumping in which the animal covers a long distance each time it moves. Certain kinds of African antelope can perform acrobatic feats of bounding.

Buck

When certain animals, such as wild horses, find a person suddenly seated on their back, they throw their hind legs violently into the air in the effort to dislodge the rider.

Canter

This is the way a horse runs at a moderate speed; it is faster than **trotting** but not so fast as **galloping**.

Dart

To move extremely fast, usually for only a short distance. This happens so quickly that often you can see the movement but not the thing that has moved.

Dash

To run as fast you can, but only over a short distance.

Frisk

To jump excitedly into the air.

Gallop

To run fast and steadily, as a horse does.

Gambol

To run about, changing direction and jumping playfully, like a couple of young dogs.

Hop

For humans, to jump on one leg; for four-footed animals, to walk with one paw raised; for small birds, to proceed in little jumps, with both feet together.

Leap

To jump once, either high in the air or, more usually, across a long distance.

Lope

To run at an easy pace, extending the legs to cover more ground with each stride. This is characteristic of wolves and large dogs and giraffes.

Pop (usually with "into" or "out of")

To enter/leave a place spontaneously or impulsively, and with no intention of staying long, especially when passing the door or because you know you can count on a ready welcome.

Pounce

To make a small jump, like a cat, in order to catch something.

Race

To run as fast as you can in order to reach a certain point before someone else or within a limited time.

Scamper

This is the way small dogs (and little children) run fast – so fast that we can hardly see the movement of the legs.

Scramble

If you are in sudden danger and can only escape by clambering up or down a slope or through a narrow aperture, or by pushing other people aside, you forget your dignity and use arms and legs, hands and feet, to reach a safe place!

Scuttle

This is the way animals with long, stiff legs, like crabs or scorpions, manage to run when in haste.

Shoot

To move like a bullet: so fast that the movement can hardly be seen.

Skip

To lift yourself off the ground in a light movement, or a series of movements. Children often do this when they feel relaxed and happy, raising one leg after the other.

Spring

When an animal such as a leopard needs to catch a prey at a certain distance, it contracts its body against its support (the ground or a tree branch) and then throws itself – like a spring released.

Vault

To jump over an obstacle, often using one or both hands to speed the action by helping to lift the body.

99 SCOFF ~ MOCK ~ JEER ~ TEASE ~ TAUNT

All these verbs mean *derision of some kind*, which is very often hurtful or even cruel.

Scoff

To *express contempt for an idea* that others take seriously, often with a laugh that does not contain real humour:

> *Everybody was so sure that the Earth was the centre of the universe that this new theory that it went round the sun was scoffed at as being completely ridiculous.*

Mock

To *imitate other people's behaviour or actions* that we find ridiculous. The intention is clearly hurtful:

> *My brother and his friends mocked my tears when my little rabbit died, which only made me feel even worse.*

Jeer

This is a mocking kind of laugh, usually with hurtful words, *intended to humiliate* the victim and enjoy his discomfiture:

> *The crowd jeered as the "tyrant" passed on his way to the guillotine.*

Tease

To use **jeering** or scorn (whether real or pretended), or repeated irritating behaviour, in order to provoke someone into an angry response:

> *They tease the animals by poking sticks at them through the bars of the cage to anger them.*

Taunt

To challenge someone to something he cannot do or to reproach him scornfully for his failings, usually in the hope of *provoking him to commit some futile act*:

> *If the other boys had not taunted Alec with cowardice, he would never have done such a stupid thing.*

100 SEEING

Seeing is involuntary – so long as our eyes are open we see without intending to; if we don't want to see something, all we can do is close our eyes. Here are some of the various ways we see when they are open. They are listed according to sense, not alphabetically.

Ways of Seeing

NOTICE ~ PERCEIVE ~ BEHOLD ~ DISCERN ~ DISTINGUISH ~ SPOT ~ SIGHT ~ GLIMPSE ~ WITNESS ~ SPY

Notice and **Perceive**

This way of seeing shows that *your attention is caught* by something or some detail in what you are looking at that makes you think about it and perhaps remember it. **Notice** is the usual verb for this; **perceive** is much more literary:

> *We noticed that his hair looked whiter than before.*

> *The judge, perceiving her distress, allowed her to remain seated.*

N.B.   It is possible to **notice** or **perceive** with any of the other senses too: the ears, the nose, the skin, etc.

Behold

This is an old-fashioned verb that describes seeing *something strange or wonderful*:

> *The shepherds, beholding a brilliant light in the sky, were filled with fear.*

Discern and Distinguish

These mean seeing something *in difficult conditions or against a difficult background* and therefore not immediately. (**Distinguish**, however, can also be used for a mental process that utilizes the intelligence instead of the eyes):

> *Looking into the darkness under the bridge, he discerned a round shape that had not been there before.*

> *The ancients distinguished planets from stars because the former moved across the firmament.*

Spot

To see something *suddenly or unexpectedly* against a confusing background. The object seen in this case is familiar or easily recognizable:

> *As the crowd of passengers streamed off the train, she spotted her sister's blond head and began waving frantically.*

Sight

Like **spot**, it means seeing suddenly, but as it is used mostly in connection with travel, what is seen is *generally some expected landmark*, especially land as viewed from the sea:

> *It was to be weeks before the crew sighted another island.*

Glimpse

To see something *too briefly to be able to perceive it well* or continue looking at it. This is a matter of circumstances: it may be that some obstacle prevents you from seeing a thing more than momentarily, or that either you or the thing is in movement and other objects between you make it impossible to keep your eyes on the thing:

> *As I raised my head, I glimpsed a figure in the passageway ahead – and then it was gone.*

> *There are so many trees surrounding the palace that you can only glimpse it between them from here, so if you really want to photograph it you'll have to go through the wood.*

Witness

To *be present when some act or action takes place* and therefore to see it all and be in a position later to certify what happened:

> *We'd like you two to witness the signing of these documents, if you don't mind.*

Spy

Another now old-fashioned verb, this stresses suddenness of seeing, so it means the same as the more modern **spot**:

> *The kind of telescope used at sea was originally called a "spyglass", because it enabled seamen to spy things that had appeared on the horizon – too far away to be seen with the naked eye.*

101 SHADE ~ SHADY ~ SHADOW ~ SHADOWY

Shade and **shadow** are essentially the same phenomenon: a patch of dark colour created by an obstacle in a strong light, but of course there are differences.

Shade (uncountable)

This is *an area* formed by some large object (a wall, a building, a tree, a mass of vegetation) that stops the sunlight. When the sun is strong we look for shade to sit in because we know it will be cool there and restful for the eyes, and as it moves relatively slowly we have plenty of time to stay there out of the sun:

> *It was now midday and getting warm, so Dennis sat down in the shade of the hedge and opened his packet of sandwiches.*

> *The sun's come out and it's hot on this pavement; let's cross the road and walk in the shade, shall we?*

A **shade** (countable) was the word used by the ancient Greeks to describe what we would call a ghost today; it is also an artistic term for variations of colour for paints, fabrics, etc.; and in compound forms it describes objects that protect us from bright light (a lampshade, an eyeshade, a sunshade ...):

My sister's had her bedroom painted a delightful shade of light green.

Shady

This is the adjective for pleasantly cool places:

We found a shady spot under some trees and took a short nap.

But when used for people, **shady** has a negative sense. It gives the idea of someone we suspect of being dishonest in some way:

His brother-in-law was a shady character, who never seemed to work but always had plenty of money to spend.

Shadow

A **shadow** (countable) is the patch of darkness created by something in the path of a strong light, not always sunlight. If the object moves, its shadow moves with it:

You can see that this photo was taken late in the afternoon because of the long shadows.

A shadow fell across my book and when I looked up it was my father, who had come to say goodnight.

We use the phrase **in shadow** to refer to a part of something that is not illuminated when there is enough light otherwise:

His face was in shadow, so I didn't recognize him at first.

In the plural, **the shadows** describes all the area that cannot be illuminated by a central light source:

I used to imagine that there were horrible things lurking in the shadows at the foot of the bed, against which my little nightlight gave me scant comfort.

Vague shapes that we guessed were hyenas came and went in the shadows beyond reach of our kerosene lamp, but none of them dared to attack us that night.

Shadowy

This is used for people, and, like **shady**, is also a negative adjective, as it describes someone we cannot see clearly and find rather sinister:

> *Before making any decision, the king always consulted his confessor, a shadowy figure that everyone feared.*

102 SHAPE ~ FORM

Shape

It describes the contour or outline of an object; that is, what we can depict in a drawing or painting. Certain shapes are so distinctive, because they are always associated with particular objects, that we can describe them by referring to those objects. Examples of these are "pear-shaped" or "egg-shaped":

> *All I could see was a silhouette, but the shape told me I was looking at some kind of reptile.*

> *There's a small model of this tower in bronze over there, for the blind to feel its shape and understand what it is that we can see.*

> *A landmark is a large object (often a building) of such a singular shape that on seeing it we recognize it at once, like the Eiffel Tower in Paris.*

Form

It is the essential material of something but has nothing to do with its contours. For instance, water exists naturally in various **forms**: as a solid (ice), as a liquid (water), and as a gas (water-vapour or atmospheric moisture):

> *Diamonds are simply carbon, but in its hardest form known.*

> *The ancient Greeks believed that their gods could appear to them in many ungodlike forms, of which that of an old man or woman was one of their favourites.*

> *Chipboard is the form of wood most employed nowadays in furniture-making on account of its cheapness.*

103 SHIP ~ BOAT ~ CRAFT ~ VESSEL

These nouns all refer to man-made objects designed originally for travel on water, and evidently there are differences between them, but even native speakers of English aren't sure what those differences are.

Ship

The essential distinction between **ship** and **boat** lies in the underwater structure: the hull (the outer casing) of a **ship** is long and relatively narrow but also deep, hanging low under the surface. **Ships** are used for *long-distance marine travel: across oceans*, where there is no risk of hitting anything under water, and the shape of the hull, with its pronounced keel, provides stability in rough seas, preventing the **ship** from overturning.

Boat

Unlike **ships**, which are never very small, **boats** can be of any size, from the small rowing boat to bulky vessels capable (as with ferries) of transporting vehicles, or heavy commercial cargoes. A **boat** is designed for use in *shallow waters* such as rivers, lakes, and coastal parts of the open sea where there is less exposure to rough or stormy weather. For this purpose the hull is much flatter than in a **ship** and the keel is greatly reduced to allow it to pass safely over the seabed or river bottom, and the deck, if there is one, is broad relative to its length.

Craft

Apart from various other meanings, which have no connection with travel at all, this is a *general term for ships and boats* of all sizes and designs, sailing on all kinds of water area. We must remember, too, that it is now also used for air and space travel (aircraft and spacecraft).

Vessel

This word too has numerous other meanings, and, as with **craft**, it serves to describe ships and boats in general, but in particular *all those used on the sea.*

104 SHOOT ~ FIRE ~ AIM ~ HIT ~ MISS

Shoot, Fire and Aim

Things we **shoot** are those that will travel fast through the air, like arrows, bullets, or cannonballs, but they can only do this when they are propelled – by a bow or some kind of gun. But notice that the bow or the gun itself does not go anywhere! If it is a bow, it is pulled; if it is a gun, it is **fired** (because the earliest guns needed fire to explode the powder they used). It is impossible to **shoot** a gun. However, it *is* possible to **shoot the victim** one has **aimed** (pointed) the gun **at**, although this does not always mean that the victim dies as a result:

> *William Tell shot the arrow right through the apple on his son's head.*
>
> *Tradition says that Harold, the last of the Anglo-Saxon kings, was shot in the eye at the Battle of Hastings.*
>
> *To fire a pistol you have to pull the trigger.*
>
> *She thought she had aimed the dart at the board, but it hit the wall several inches to one side.*

Hit and Miss

If you have aimed the gun right and then you fire it, you will probably **hit** the objective, leaving a bullet-hole in it. But if your aim was bad or your hand shook, you will **miss** (not hit) it. The same consequences can happen if you throw a stone at something or try to punch someone: you either **hit** or **miss** it or him.

Also, if a vehicle such as a tank is driven aggressively, in order to attack and damage an enemy vehicle, the enemy will naturally try to escape the charge, so the attacker may **miss** (find that the enemy has just moved out of danger).

Transferring this to a different, non-belligerent situation, we have the familiar case of someone who wants to *catch* a vehicle leaving or passing at a certain moment, or is *hoping to be present* at an occasion that has a fixed moment; if he is too slow or too late, he will **miss** that (train) or **miss** the (ceremony).

105 SIGN ~ SIGNAL

Both of these are a *clear indication* (something we see or hear and understand at once) that gives us useful or important information, so what is the difference?

Sign

Signs, which are manifestations of change, fall into four classes:

1. Static signs are simply *a change of circumstances* – something new from which we deduce what has happened, what is happening, or what is going to happen (in a law court this would be called "evidence"):

    A rumpled bed is a sign that somebody has used the bed fairly recently.

    The next day there was still no sign of improvement in her condition and everyone was getting seriously worried.

    This carpet is beginning to show signs of wear.

    A build-up of dark clouds is a sign of an impending storm.

    Cover your geraniums at the first sign of frost.

2. Involuntary movements (a look, a change of expression or posture, a gasp, flushing, sweating...) are signs that *reveal something*:

    Yawning is a sure sign that the audience is losing interest in a talk.

    The way his eyes lit up when Sarah came in was a most satisfactory sign to her mother, who was watching him keenly.

    A cat's tail twitching from side to side is a sign that something has caught the animal's attention.

3. Voluntary movements are signs we make with parts of the body (eyes, eyebrows, mouth, hands,...) *to communicate feelings or impressions*, or to prompt a response:

    At this, he removed his glasses and stared at me, which I interpreted as a sign that my words had made an impact.

    She looked round suddenly and caught him making vulgar signs to his cronies.

4. But there are material signs, too; pictorial symbols *made to convey a permanent specific message*, like these:

- a tick on a document (a sign that something has been approved);
- warning signs, such as a skull or a representation of lightning;
- painted arrows, shop signs, road signs, signboards, etc.

The important thing is that signs, even movement signs, don't actually move or change position.

Signal

Like a **sign**, a **signal** has to be seen, heard, or felt. But a **signal** is also a movement, not something static, and it is made specifically *for immediate action*: to tell people who have been waiting for this that the time has come to act. It tells them what to do next or how to proceed. This means that it must be instantly recognised as having this function – as being a signal and not an accidental movement:

> *If your car's indicator lights fail to work you will have to rely on hand signals.*
>
> *The amber traffic light was intended only as a signal for preparation, not for accelerating at once.*
>
> *It had been agreed that a single shot should be the signal for starting the attack.*
>
> *She poked him hard in the back as a signal to enter the discussion, but he was too shy to say a word.*

The corresponding verb is **to signal** (= to make a signal). There is also a rather literary adjective **signal**, but it means *exceptional*:

> *The company has made signal progress in the software field.*

106 SINCERE ~ HONEST ~ TRUTHFUL ~ CANDID ~ FRANK

Here are five rather confusing adjectives, all referring to things people say and how or why they are said. (**Honest** can also be used to describe behaviour). But let's see what other differences there are between them.

Sincere

A sincere person is one who *really feels what he says or shows* in his facial or bodily expression, and so sincere language is what really reflects the feelings of the speaker.

Its opposite is *insincere*, which means not that the speaker is lying but that what he says is not what he feels at heart, or that his attitude is not genuine.

Honest

An honest person not only has no intention of deceiving (or therefore of lying) when in the circumstances one might well expect this, but is *incapable of deceit altogether*. Honest behaviour (that is, actions), being free from all attempt at deceit, can be trusted completely. The opposite is *dishonest*: the person is trying to deceive.

Truthful

A truthful person *does not lie* or even try to lie; so truthful words tell exactly what the facts are. Its opposite is *untruthful*, meaning that what is said is a lie or distorts the facts in some way.

Candid and Frank

There is scarcely any difference between these: a candid (frank) person gives his *true opinion* without regard for the listener's feelings. A candid or frank answer consequently states exactly what the speaker thinks, no matter whether it pleases or hurts. These words have no opposite forms.

107 SOON ~ QUICKLY

What these adverbs have in common is that they show approval – we are happy with the situation. The difference is this:

Soon

This is used when an action is going to take place a short time after the moment in question (which may be a present or past one). It indicates the *resulting situation* and stresses that *we shall not have to wait long*.

Quickly

Instead of referring to the time of the action, **quickly** stresses *the speed at which that action takes place*.

So now look at this example:

> *They worked quickly and so the job was soon done.*

This tells us that the people concerned, realising how important the job was, *wasted no time* in doing it, and there was thus *a minimum of delay*. The job was finished to everyone's satisfaction.

Special points

1. When the doer of the action is not a person, either word can be used:

    > *Once the weather had turned sunny, the flowers soon/quickly began to open.*

2. If you want to show that you don't want the situation to change, because you are enjoying it as it is, use *all-too* **quickly/soon**:

    > *The afternoon seemed to pass in no time and all-too soon they had to set off homewards once more.*

3. The normal position for **soon** is before the main part of the verb, but **quickly** is positioned according to what we want to emphasise: after the verb to *stress the speed of the action*, and before it to *stress the urgency of the action*:

I'll have to show you round the house rather quickly, because I've got to go and meet some more visitors in a few minutes.

Seeing his mistake, he quickly apologised and repeated the request.

Other general examples

You'd better start collecting your bags: we shall soon be arriving at our destination.

Quickly outlining her plan, she left us to talk it over.

I had to shut the door quickly in case the dogs escaped.

We were impressed by how quickly they cleared up the mess, and how soon the place was tidy again.

Spring is coming; the trees will soon be in leaf.

108 SPECIAL ~ ESPECIAL ~ SPECIALLY ~ ESPECIALLY

These are all very similar words, and they are from the same origin, but (when used correctly, which is not often nowadays) they don't mean the same thing.

Special

This adjective is used mostly with common nouns. A simple definition is "different"; that is, different from all other, more ordinary, cases. In this way, a **special** bed differs from all other beds, and it is different because this bed was *made for a certain purpose* (*or for a certain person*, who demanded or needed unusual characteristics in the bed). In other words, it was designed in this form because there was a need for it. And because something is **special**, it is also considered more important:

A retirement home is a kind of private hotel with special facilities for retired people.

The Pope travels about in a special vehicle, in which he can be clearly seen but is protected from possible assassination attempts.

"I have several grandchildren, but you are very special to me, dear", said my grandmother.

The doctor warned me that I would need special help for several weeks until my eyesight was back to normal.

Especial

This time the adjective is used exclusively with abstract nouns. And again, a simple definition is "more..." – that is, *more than usual of whatever is being described*. So we read our favourite section in the newspaper with **especial** interest; that is, our interest is greater than in other cases:

> *The weekly arrival of the stagecoach always aroused especial excitement in the village.*

> *Highly conscious of his patient's importance, the surgeon operated with especial concentration and thoroughness.*

(Some authorities consider that the distinction between these words is so fine that it is unnecessary these days to maintain it and therefore **special** may be used correctly instead of **especial**).

Specially

You will find this adverb used only in conjunction with verbs, where it tells us that the action described *would never have occurred had the need for it not existed*. Thus, we say that something was designed, planned, made, executed, performed, etc. **specially** when the need for it became evident:

> *What a nuisance! I went all that way specially to see the exhibition, and when I got there it was over!*

> *Do you realize that the floor would have to be specially strengthened if you decided on such heavy furniture?*

Especially

This word is often used with an adjective or another adverb, or with a verb, with the meaning of *unusually*. It very often appears at the beginning of an additional phrase to mean *more so*, and is the same as saying *in particular*:

> *It must have been especially cold last night because the frost has killed all the young plants we had just put in.*

> *She was especially confused by his use of technical language to describe something already complicated to understand.*

> *It gets very crowded here in the evening, especially at weekends.*

109 SUBSTITUTE ~ REPLACE

The first of these verbs has both a different use and a significantly different meaning in English from its counterpart in other European languages. But let's begin with **replace**, which is easier to understand.

Replace

This verb, which takes the preposition *with* (or possibly *by* in the passive), means *to put something new or needed in the place of something old or unwanted*. Consequently, when a change is required we **replace** the existing thing **with** (or **by** in a passive phrase) what we want to have instead (its replacement) – that is, we **replace** x **with** y. Moreover, there is a strong sense of *improvement* here:

> *The town is planning to replace the damaged monument with an illuminated fountain.*

> *Nobody wants to replace the traditional cable-cars in San Francisco.*
> Nothing can be better than the cable-cars.

> *The ancient despotism was eventually replaced* (passive!) *by a democratic republic.*

Substitute

It is followed by the preposition *for*, but what is difficult is to understand that in this case the order of parts is reversed – we **substitute** something new **for** the previous thing (we **substitute** y **for** x this time) – and also that very often there is no improvement in this change; in fact, the replacement (the substitute) may well be *inferior*:

> *When butter became unobtainable, the army substituted margarine, and it was a universally unpopular choice.*

> *Plastic has been substituted for glass in the packaging of bottled water. It is certainly much cheaper but is ecologically less recommendable.*

> *In following his publisher's advice to simplify the plot of his novel, he found he had merely substituted expediency for literary quality.*

110 SURE ~ SAFE ~ SECURE

These three adjectives are often expressed in a single word in other languages, which means that the distinctions between them are a problem for those speakers.

Sure

We use this to describe *an attitude of mind*. When we have no doubt and regard a fact as *certain*, we are **sure** about it, or it is **sure** (in our opinion) to happen. If we have been asked to do something, agree to something, or concede something that the other person secretly considers excessive, and we say "yes", that person may well need confirmation, saying "Are you sure?" (In other words, "I hope you've really thought about this"):

> *I'm sure he said he was going on holiday last week.*
>
> *Are you quite sure it's all right if I come too?*
>
> *Mike's sure to like you – he can't resist blue-eyed girls!*

Safe

This describes a physical condition – that *there is no danger to the health or to the existence or life* of something or someone:

> *Safe sex means using some form of protection against infection.*
>
> *Keep your jewels in a safe place such as a bank vault.*
>
> *Babies are never safe in a car unless strapped in.*

Secure

This also means *out of danger*, but here the danger is circumstantial rather than physical: not that the thing concerned can be harmed but that it *cannot be lost or get out of place*. Consequently, we use this word to talk about things in precarious positions or that can break away and get lost, like buttons, wigs, small boats – and reputations:

> *That button doesn't look very secure to me; why don't you pull it right off and put in your pocket?*

On the other hand, both **safe** and **secure** can be used – although of course with their different meanings – for places and positions of all kinds (including jobs).

For instance, a **safe** job is one that doesn't involve any physical danger; a **secure** job is one that the worker expects to keep all his life. Likewise, a **safe** position is one in which there is no danger: one cannot be attacked; a **secure** position is the kind that one cannot lose – in the sense that one cannot fall from it.

The opposites of all these are respectively *unsure, unsafe* and *insecure*.

111 SURE (TO) ~ CERTAIN (TO) ~ BOUND TO

1. *Function:* all these three adjectives usually come after the verb "to be" and are followed by the infinitive of the operative verb – or, in the case of **sure** and **certain**, by a clause:

    It's sure/certain/bound to rain this weekend.

    Are you quite sure/certain (that) she said she was going out for the day?

    He'd better be sure/certain how much he is ready to pay before he chooses the article.

2. *Meaning:* none of them means *real certainty*. They all show a certainty that exists only as a belief – in the mind of the speaker, of course. If we know that something is certain, we say so as a fact, without using one of these words:

    I love you!   (To use, say, **I'm sure** here would not sound at all convincing!)

Sure and certain

These two words (which are virtually the same in meaning) indicate a believed certainty which is *based on logic and calculated probability*:

Leave it pinned to the door; they're sure (certain) to see it as soon as they come in.

Bound to (+ infinitive)

This expresses a similarly believed certainty, but this time *based on the speaker's experience of this situation*, and it often reveals scepticism or irony:

> *There's bound to be a crowd of reporters waiting for us.*
> The speaker has probably experienced this kind of situation before or knows of similar cases.

> *For goodness sake, don't take that new umbrella: with your memory you're bound to leave it behind somewhere!*
> We can expect an absent-minded person like you to do that!

112 SYMPATHY ~ COMPASSION ~ PITY

Sympathy

This is a kind and very human feeling, how we feel towards someone who is suffering. Perhaps we have suffered the same thing and know exactly what that person is going through, perhaps we can only imagine the suffering, but because *the other person is like us – an equal –* we are sorry they are undergoing such unhappiness:

> *Martha watched the other woman's clumsy walk with full sympathy: she too had had a difficult time towards the end of her last pregnancy.*

Compassion

It is no less kind, but it is the feeling of someone who is in such *a superior position* that he or she will never personally experience the other's suffering. It is the kind of feeling we attribute notably to non-mortals, who are of course free of the calamities that afflict human beings:

> *Looking down with compassion on her hero's anguish, Aphrodite at last resolved to intervene and rescue him.*

Pity

It is not a kind feeling, and for this reason it is so often resented. It is our attitude towards someone in trouble for whom *we feel no particular affection,* or someone who perhaps *deserves part of what he is suffering:*

As his kidnappers were handcuffed and taken away, Aubrey reflected with some pity that they could expect little mercy from the local police.

Words associated with these are the adjectives **sympathetic** and **compassionate**, and the verbs **to sympathize (with)** and **to pity**:

Don't take Julian seriously when he says that since his divorce he sympathizes with married men.

I pity those workmen, having to carry on in such bitterly cold weather.

There is also the special adjective **pitiful**, which we use to describe a very poor effort or some calamitous state, particularly when it is the sufferer who is responsible for that state:

Clearly, what Will had done was serious indeed, and the others listened in silence to his pitiful attempts to justify himself.

113 TAKING
(Ways of taking what is not yours)

English contains an impressive list of verbs that mean different ways of obtaining things that belong to other people, from the most elementary verbs (see separate entry under **Rob, Steal**) to the most modern and sophisticated versions of these basic actions.

Here are some variations (in alphabetic order) on the **stealing** theme (bear in mind that at the time the victim is unaware of what is happening):

ABSCOND ~ CHEAT ~ "CON" ~ EMBEZZLE ~ FILCH ~ MISAPPROPRIATE ~ PILFER ~ PLAGIARIZE ~ POACH ~ PURLOIN ~ RUSTLE ~ SHOPLIFT ~ SHORT-CHANGE ~ SWINDLE ~ THIEVE

Abscond

Normally to hide from authority, but when followed by "with", it means that something (usually money) has been taken too:

The press reported that the minister had absconded with the special fund entrusted to him.

Cheat

To give someone inferior value or less quantity that he has paid for, or (with "of") to leave him without his rightful possessions by some false means:

Look at this! That man in the market has cheated me: these apples are nothing like the beautiful ones he had on display!

The winner was cheated of his prize by a legal quibble.

"Con"

(Familiar form). To cheat by first gaining the victim's confidence:

My neighbour was conned by two men posing as technicians, who induced her to let them "repair" her television aerial, and then overcharged her shockingly.

Embezzle

To steal money entrusted to one, usually these days by transferring it to a different account:

The secretary of the charity was imprisoned for embezzling funds destined for third-world countries. He had put them into an account in Switzerland.

Filch

To steal objects of little value or trivial amounts of cash:

All the small change I had left on the bench in the club dressing-room was filched while I was showering yesterday.

Misappropriate

A business legal term meaning to use for your own benefit other people's money entrusted to your care:

He has been accused of misappropriating the Association's capital while he was treasurer.

Pilfer

Like **filch**, to steal things of very little value:

Children are always pilfering chewing-gum and sweets from the poor woman's stall, but she doesn't seem to mind.

Plagiarize

To steal another person's ideas and present them as your own:

Famous industrial names are being plagiarized by certain unscrupulous firms in this part of the world, which is very hard to prosecute at such a distance.

Poach

To enter a private area in order to capture or kill animals kept or being bred there by the landowner:

Elephants in this nature reserve are constantly being poached: killed solely for their tusks.

Purloin

To obtain dishonestly, especially when it is something entrusted to you:

How did they manage to purloin such quantities of bonds?

Rustle

To steal another man's cattle. This verb developed – and is used mainly – in the USA, where such actions were at one time fairly common:

Fifty thousand head of cattle were rustled in this valley on one occasion.

Shoplift

To specialize in stealing goods from shops:

We lose far more articles through shoplifting than through normal breakage in this store.

Short-change

To return less than should be given when changing money:

> *I'm never going back to that shop again; they've tried to short-change me twice this month.*

Swindle

It means the same as **cheat**, but is used when the victim feels particularly indignant:

> *I thought that firm was trustworthy, but they swindled me out of a lot of money in the sale of my bungalow.*

Thieve

It's similar to **steal**, but likely to be used of animals instead of humans:

> *Rossini wrote this overture for an opera called "The Thieving Magpie".*

Different ways of **robbing** (note that this crime affects either buildings that house valuable objects, or a human victim who, unfortunately, knows that it is happening to him):

ABDUCT ~ BLACKMAIL ~ BURGLE ~ HIJACK ~ KIDNAP ~ LOOT ~ MUG ~ PLUNDER ~ SACK

Abduct

To take, and keep, a person away from their spouse or family, no matter with what motive:

> *The ancient Romans, in need of wives, abducted women from the Sabine tribe.*

Blackmail

To compel someone to pay money under threat of making public something that person wants desperately to keep secret:

> *The man who had stolen the letters to her lover blackmailed her for months by threatening to send them to her husband.*

Burgle

To enter someone else's premises by night and take things:

> *She told me that they had been burgled four times, yet the burglars had never discovered her pearls.*

Hijack

To occupy a public vehicle of transport (bus, plane, ship, etc.) by force for your own private purposes:

> *Halfway across Africa, the plane was hijacked by terrorists posing as passengers, who tried to induce the pilot to fly them to a country more sympathetic to their cause.*

Kidnap

Like **abduct**, to take someone away, but in this case the purpose is to obtain money or political concessions:

> *Taking the threats to kidnap a member of his family seriously, the millionaire hired bodyguards to watch his wife and children, but forgot himself.*

Loot

To take advantage of some state of disaster like an earthquake to help yourself to other people's (unprotected) property. It is included under **robbing** because it is the home or shop that is looted, not the objects stolen:

> *Looters had started smashing shop windows even before the bombed town had been fully evacuated.*

Mug

To stop or attack someone in the street and demand their possessions, usually under threat of immediate injury:

> *So many tourists have been mugged in this part of the city this summer that special police have been brought in.*

Plunder

Like **loot**, to take all you can from a defenceless place, but in this case the place is typically a conquered town and the plunderers are the invading troops:

Although the fort surrendered at once, the commander allowed his men to plunder it as a warning to others.

Sack

It's an alternative to **plunder**, also used of captured towns or palaces, but more thoroughly done:

The usual fate of any town that resisted conquest was to be sacked by the victors and its inhabitants killed or enslaved.

114 TALL ~ HIGH ~ LOW ~ HEIGHT ~ TALLNESS

It is necessary to distinguish only the first two of these adjectives. Both can serve to measure the upwards distance to the top of something, but here are the differences.

Tall (opposite: short)

Use this to describe a standing object, one that is *vertically long but horizontally narrow*, so in many cases we have to look up it to see the top, as with a tower. Other objects we describe as **tall** are trees, posts, chimneys, standing clocks, and of course human beings:

My grandfather's clock was taller by far than the old man himself.

Sequoias are the tallest trees in the world.

How tall is your brother Jim?

So we use **tall** when the relative narrowness of an object is more important than its other dimensions.

High (opposite: low)

This is much more widely used, because it can describe more kinds of object and other situations. There are four cases in which **high** is used:

1. For objects *standing on or forming part of the ground*, such as doorsteps, most articles of furniture, vehicles, most buildings, walls of all kinds, large waves, and topographic features like cliffs, hills, and mountains. **High** refers here to the distance between the base and the top:

Careful! This step is a fraction higher than the other ones.

That chair is rather low; wouldn't you prefer a higher one?

The film is about a hill that wasn't quite high enough to be called a mountain.

Extremely rough sea is expected tomorrow, with waves of over seven metres high.

2. For things that are *situated or suspended above the ground*, such as rooftops, lamps, ceilings, doorways (the top of the doorway), windows, tree branches, balloons, flying aircraft, clouds, and the various layers of the Earth's atmosphere. In this case **high** describes their distance from the ground:

> *The chandelier was high, but he was so tall that it brushed his head as he passed under it.*
>
> *The bright object turned out to be a meteorological balloon flying high over the town.*
>
> *The best apples are on branches that are too high for the pickers to reach.*

3. For the *forehead* (or brow) in the human face:

> *In a high forehead the hairline is well separated from the eyebrows.*

(What all these examples have in common is that *besides being high, these objects are also wide* – sometimes even wider than high, which is quite the contrary with **tall**).

4. For estimating *rate of growth*:

> *"The corn is as high as an elephant's eye". From the musical "Oklahoma".*
>
> *"I remember Dad telling me about his life on the sea when I was only this high",* said Tom, holding his hand at knee level.

The usual noun for both adjectives is **height**; **tallness** is very uncommon.

115 TOWN ~ COUNTRY ~ COUNTRYSIDE ~ LANDSCAPE

Town

When **town** is contrasted with **country** we are thinking of two concepts of living-styles.

Although **town** in this sense refers particularly to the capital city, it is also used for *any fully urbanised area*: streets lined with buildings, and very little planted vegetation other than in parks and public gardens. We use the word in the singular and without any article, as in phrases like **to be in town, to come / go to town**, or we make an adjective of it, as in **town life, a town house**, and (in the USA) **to go downtown.**

Country

The country means everything else: *mainly open land* but including the roads, villages, and isolated buildings found there. The largest of these are national roads – links between cities, but when roads are obviously made and kept by local authorities we call them **country roads**. We also use the oxymoron **a country town** to mean any small town situated at a distance from the principal ones.

Countryside

The countryside is not a place at all, but an impression – what we see: the *appearance of the country* when we travel through it. Consequently it is illogical to talk about "going to the countryside" or "living in the countryside". Instead, we comment on aspects like "the beauty of the countryside".

Bear in mind that this word refers essentially to the low-lying and extensively cultivated lands between towns, typical of much of central and western Europe.

Landscape

If we want to describe more *rugged and more spectacular areas* (especially with mountains or large hills and valleys or gorges), with little sign of human habitation, such as can be seen in wilder parts of the world, this is the right word.

116 TROUBLE ~ TO TROUBLE ~ NUISANCE ~ BOTHER

Trouble

This noun, which is almost always uncountable, implies some negative situation that is in most cases unexpected. Its precise meaning varies according to the circumstances, however. Here are some typical instances of its use:

1. *To be too much (or no) trouble* stresses the degree of inconvenience that some action causes:

    It's too much trouble to write letters when you can phone, don't you think?

    Brian said it would be no trouble for him to collect the mail for me every day, which I thought was very kind.

2. *To have trouble with adult people* indicates a disruption of the normal relations and probably some animosity:

    I've had no trouble with my new neighbours so far. They seem to be very nice people.

3. *To have trouble with children* (or other inferiors) means that they are not behaving as well as before:

    We had a lot of trouble with our maid when she decided to go on a slimming diet and became very bad-tempered.

4. *To have trouble with mechanical objects* (and this includes parts of the body) describes some malfunction:

He had no end of trouble with his old car, but he says the new one is a delight to drive.

5. *To give (someone) trouble* is used of the part that we are complaining about:

    Her dentures began giving her trouble the day they were fitted.

6. *To be in trouble* (with the authorities) shows that someone has done wrong and is liable to be punished for it:

    Their son is always getting into trouble over his poor attendance at school.

7. *To cause trouble* describes behaviour that is deliberately provocative, especially against some kind of authority:

    Those refugees who had begun causing trouble soon after their arrival in the camp, protesting about the food and accommodation, were quickly repatriated.

8. *To make trouble* refers to behaviour intended to disrupt good relations between people:

    Although she herself was good at her job, she was eventually dismissed for making trouble among her fellow workers, setting one against another.

The adjective to describe whatever or whoever is causing trouble is **troublesome**:

The worst of living in a flat is the risk of having troublesome next-door neighbours.

Many of the host families found the children they had adopted to be very troublesome as a result of their early experiences in the orphanage.

To trouble

As an intransitive verb, **to trouble** is a synonym of **to bother** (see next page), and is likewise used in the negative or interrogative.

The transitive **to trouble someone** means *to make it necessary for a person to do things that he or she would not otherwise have to do*:

I'm sorry to trouble you, but you're sitting on my coat.
= means that the person spoken to will have to get up.

To **take the trouble** means *to spontaneously do something (for another person) that one would not normally do*. It is thus the exact opposite of **not to bother**:

> *The librarian kindly took the trouble to telephone me at home when the book I wanted was finally available.*

Another similar verbal phrase is **to go to trouble**:

> *Her friends went to a lot of trouble to find her a suitable escort for the party.*

Nuisance

This word is the specific – and countable – equivalent of **trouble**, with the characteristic that it suggests that the speaker is not only inconvenienced but greatly irritated by the thing described:

> *It's a nuisance to have to ring the bell every time, just because I haven't been given a key yet.*

Bother

This noun means much the same as **trouble**, but the inconvenience is greater:

> *Some children find it too much bother to clean their teeth properly – and they suffer for it later in life.*

To bother, *used in the negative (and sometimes in the interrogative)*, means not to do something because the person considers it needless effort:

> *He told me where to look, but he didn't bother to get up and show me.*

117 UNDOUBTEDLY ~ WITHOUT DOUBT ~ DOUBTLESS ~ NO DOUBT ~ I'M SURE

Undoubtedly and Without doubt

At first sight all these adverbs, whose function is to convince, must mean the same, but in practice there is an important distinction: only the first two mean literally what they express – that the matter is certain:

Columbus was undoubtedly / without doubt a man of decision and courage; without these qualities he could never have carried out the mission of discovery that he had set himself.

Doubtless, No doubt and I'm sure

They all imply that there is in fact an element of doubt, which is the *opposite of what they seem to mean.* (**Doubtless** is the most formal of these and **I'm sure** is the most hopeful):

Doubtless many of you are already wondering where the money for this ambitious project is coming from.
Although the speaker cannot be at all sure of this fact, it is on his mind because he is probably anticipating some awkward questions about the financing of the project and is most likely intending to answer them before they can be raised!

No doubt you realize now how foolish you've been, Eddie, and perhaps you're sorry you did it.
Here the speaker is probably hoping to influence the boy, who may or may not be as repentant as he implies.

I'm sure everybody here will be delighted to know that the local planning authority has just given us the go-ahead to start building our welfare centre.
The speaker is evidently one of the most enthusiastic supporters of this scheme!

118 UNEXPECTED APPLICATIONS
(Familiar words used in unexpected ways)

**ADDRESS ~ ALLOW ~ DEAL ~ DELIVER ~ DRAW ~ GAME ~
GIVE ~ HOLD ~ INFORM ~ MEET ~ SHOOT ~ TELL ~
TELLING ~ TRY ~ TRYING ~ WORK**

Address

As a transitive verb, besides the familiar action of putting the address on a letter, we can also (in more formal situations) address a problem: that is, *deal with* it:

This is a matter we shall have to address at once.

As a noun it means *a formal speech*:

> *The Pope made no reference to the protests in his address.*

Allow (+ **for**)

Besides meaning *permit*, if this is followed by "for" it means *take into consideration*:

> *We allow for growth when buying shoes for children.*
> We buy larger sizes than they need now because their feet will soon grow and need larger shoes.

Deal

You probably know "to deal with" as meaning *conduct business*, but without any preposition it means either *distribute* to everyone (esp. playing-cards) or *hit someone*:

> *The traditional way to deal the cards is clockwise round the table: from left to right.*
>
> *My father used to deal me a hard slap every time he saw my elbows on the table.*

Deliver

Besides delivering the expected things like letters or the morning milk, we can deliver a baby (*help it to be born by releasing it from its mother*), or (like **deal** above) deliver *something unwanted like a punch*:

> *A midwife is as expert at delivering babies as a doctor is.*
>
> *The first boxer now delivered a couple of fast blows to the stomach that left his opponent helpless.*

Draw

We can draw a picture (with a pencil), draw (*attract discreetly or even unintentionally*) someone's attention, or draw (*arrive at*) a conclusion:

> *Their noisy laughter drew the attention of the museum attendant.*

(Also see **Pulling**)

Game

As the familiar countable noun it means a *fun activity*, but the uncountable equivalent refers to *animals that people can pursue for the enjoyment of killing them*. The important aspect is that they are not killed for food but for sport. **Big game** refers to large, probably dangerous animals such as elephants or tigers; small animals are called **small game**:

> *The Scottish moors are famous for their game, which draws many prosperous tourists every shooting season.*

Give

The unfamiliar meaning is *yield (not support a weight or pressure)*:

> *There was quite a depression in the middle of the floor, where it was giving under the weight of so much furniture.*

Hold

Besides holding material objects (in, say, the hand), we can hold non-physical things, such as *an opinion or a position of responsibility*:

> *Stan holds some strange views on women's lib!*

> *For over twenty years he held the post of butler in an aristocratic home, so he knows a lot about wines.*

We also hold *all kinds of meetings*, including assemblies, parties, and courts, both royal and juridical:

> *The wedding ceremony will be held at St Margaret's Church.*

> *The first time court was held at Madrid was under Philip II.*

And it can indicate *capacity*:

> *The reception room will hold up to fifty people comfortably.*

Inform

Apart from meaning *notify*, this verb sometimes means *give form or some special quality to*:

> *Good taste informed all his work.*

Meet

Besides the common use of **meeting** a friend, this verb means *satisfy* (for situations like a need, a demand, or someone's expectations):

> *Your latest deliveries have not fully met our requirements.*

Shoot

When a plant shoots, it begins to *grow quickly* after a period of inaction such as winter. A **shoot** (noun) is *a new growing part* that has appeared above ground or on a tree branch at these times:

> *After so much rain, and now this sunshine, the garden will start shooting everywhere. Look, there's a first little shoot on this tree already!*

Tell (trans. verb)

Besides telling someone a story or telling the time, we can tell (*pass through the fingers, as if counting*) objects like beads on a string, e.g. a rosary.

Tell (intrans. verb)

To show some (usually negative) *kind of effect*:

> *The strain on them all was beginning to tell – they looked pale and tired now.*

This verb can also have a transitive form with "on", and with the same meaning as above:

> *Such a hard life had told on him, for at forty-five he looked like an old man.*

Telling (adjective)

This is the adjective from the above verb, so it means *showing consequences* (and is often used in the phrase **telling effect**):

> *These fresh reinforcements joined the battle with telling vigour: the enemy began to yield ground before their onslaught.*

Try

Apart from its usual meaning, *make an attempt*, this verb often means *test something to see how good it is*:

> *Would you like to try one of these cakes? I'm sure you'll like them.*

But it can also mean *see how much suffering someone will take*:

> *The children's behaviour tried my patience to the limit.*

Trying (adjective)

This comes from the last use of **try**, so similarly it means *testing someone's endurance*:

> *She had a terribly trying time in the months following her husband's death, and it's amazing that she survived so well.*

Work

This is not the common intransitive verb, which describes a way of earning money, but a more elementary notion, meaning:

1. *To use effort in order to create an effect* (such as a miracle):

> *That new drug has worked wonders for my rheumatism.*

2. *To extract minerals* from things like mines or quarries:

> *Our sandpits have not been worked since the Middle Ages.*

3. *To manipulate or transform* a material (such as wood or metal):

> *The Incas were masters at working gold.*

4. *To cultivate land*:

> *We shall need many more labourers to work all these fields.*

119 VIEW ~ VIEWPOINT ~ OPINION ~ ATTITUDE ~ OUTLOOK ~ MANNER ~ BEHAVIOUR

View

A **view**, in the literal sense, is what we see spread out before us as far as our eyes can reach. But figuratively it is our individual *way of seeing something*, usually a situation, *without being personally involved*. The preposition is *in*:

> *In my view, you are making a big mistake, but I presume you've thought about it and know what you're doing.*

Likewise, **to view** means *to look at a situation in a personal way*:

> *John viewed the situation rather pessimistically because of what he saw might happen to him.*

Viewpoint (Point of view)

This is the position, when **viewing** a situation, of someone who is *involved personally and will be affected* by it. Individual positions differ, so each **viewer** sees that situation rather differently. The preposition needed is *from*:

> *From my point of view as a parent, the education system doesn't take the child's home background sufficiently into account, but I can see how a teacher would look at it.*

Opinion

Whereas a **view** is a way of seeing a case and a **viewpoint** is the personal position for looking at it, an **opinion** is more than those: it is a judgement; that is, someone has *considered a situation and come to a conclusion about it*. We first *form* and then *hold* an opinion. And the preposition is *in*:

> *In my opinion, we ought to start cutting costs now.*
> I have thought about this and here is my contribution.

Attitude

An **attitude** is a kind of *mental preparation for our expectations*. That is, if you expect a certain thing to happen, you *adopt* an **attitude** in readiness; someone who is expecting opposition to his plans adopts an attitude of wariness. If the expected thing does not happen, his attitude changes accordingly:

> *I was surprised at the man's attitude: he seemed to think I was going to attack him and was on the defensive from the beginning.*
> He had prepared himself for antagonism.

Outlook

An **outlook** can be described as someone's **attitude**, not to other people but *to life in general, or to a particular aspect* of life:

One could say that your outlook on life is a basically positive one: you seek out the best in every opportunity.

Manner

If an **attitude** is not obvious at first, it becomes clear from the person's **manner**; that is, his way of *showing his thoughts* about another person. For instance, a wary attitude is shown by a cool, reserved, or tense manner.

Manner is displayed in many ways: in the expression of the face, in the tone of voice, and even in the posture of the body (which is also called an **attitude**):

> *Her manner was once again as friendly as it used to be: she smiled and greeted me warmly as soon as she saw me, and I realized that she had quite forgiven me.*

Behaviour

If our attitude to a person or a circumstance is expressed by our **manner**, it is revealed even more clearly by *the things we do*: by our **behaviour** – in how we move, what we say, etc.

> *Dogs express their feelings most clearly through their behaviour.*

> *Charlie's behaviour all the rest of the evening showed how annoyed he was at not winning the game. He sat alone in one corner and refused to take part in anything else.*

120 WAIT ~ EXPECT ~ HOPE

In some other languages the meanings of these three verbs are expressed by only one, which makes these especially problematic for non-English speakers.

Wait

This verb means *let time pass until a certain thing happens* (and there is no doubt in the mind that it will happen). It can be followed either:

1. by a place:

> *You're waiting at the wrong place, you know; the bus-stop has been moved to the next street-corner.*

2. by an object with "for":

    Do you think we'll have to wait long for the others?

    They sat there in silence, waiting for the dawn.

3. by an infinitive verb:

    There's a group of his fans outside, waiting to catch a glimpse of their idol.

4. by both object and infinitive:

    I think I'd better wait for the boss to finish dictating before asking him about that week's holiday.

5. or by a unit of time, even though "for" is not strictly necessary in this case:

    Where have you been all this time? I've been waiting here (for) over an hour.

Expect

In this case there is no certainty, but logic, or our knowledge of the situation, tells us that a certain thing will probably happen, so it is *a reasonable and logical assumption*. It is followed either:

1. by an object alone, when there is a second (omitted) verb that can easily be inferred:

    Oh, it's you! I was expecting (to see) my husband.

2. by an infinitive verb (which may have its own object):

    People can expect to live to well over seventy these days.

    Expecting to find a middle-aged person in charge, she was taken aback by the extreme youth of the police sergeant.

3. or by a "that..." clause:

    Nobody would have expected that things would turn out like this!

When **expect** is followed by an object plus infinitive, there are two interpretations. It may mean *a logical assumption* (as above):

Everyone had expected the hotel to provide a packed lunch.

I expected the man to apologize, but he just walked away.

or it *places responsibility for something on the other person*:

> *I expect you to behave more sensibly from now on, Harry.*

> *She was expected to do all the nasty jobs that nobody else would take on, so of course she soon gave notice.*

Hope

This time neither certainty nor logic is involved. It is a question of basic emotion: *wanting something to happen*, no matter how reasonable or not this desire may be. **Hope** is not followed by an object but

1. by an infinitive verb:

> *So depressed was she that day after day she hoped not to wake up the next morning.*

2. or by a "that..." clause:

> *He had secretly been hoping that somebody would remember his birthday.*

121 WALKING
(Ways of Walking)

There are very many different ways of walking and many reasons for these, as each of the following verbs describes.

AMBLE ~ BUSTLE ~ CREEP ~ DAWDLE ~ EDGE ~ FLOUNCE ~ HOBBLE ~ LAG ~ LIMP ~ LINGER ~ MARCH ~ MINCE ~ PACE ~ PAD ~ PLOD ~ PROWL ~ RAMBLE ~ SAUNTER ~ SHUFFLE ~ SIDLE ~ SLIP ~ STAGGER ~ STEAL ~ STEP ~ STRIDE ~ STROLL ~ STRUT ~ SWAGGER ~ TIPTOE ~ TODDLE ~ TRAIPSE ~ TROT ~ TRUDGE ~ WADDLE ~ WADE

Amble

To walk fairly slowly, often stopping, in a relaxed way, simply because *there is no need for haste*:

> *After lunch he ambled round to the pub to see if any of his friends were available for a chat.*

Bustle (usually with "along" or "about")

To walk energetically or move from place to place quickly *because you have a lot of things to do*:

> *I found her bustling about the house, dusting and polishing every room with all her usual vigour.*

Creep

To move *slowly and carefully enough not to be seen or heard.* We do this particularly when someone else is asleep. (Compare it with **steal**.):

> *I'll just leave it here for you to look at later, and then creep out without another word, as you're so busy.*

> *Father Christmas crept into the children's room to put their presents on the bed for the next morning.*

Dawdle

To walk as slowly as you can, using every excuse to stop, because you *don't want to arrive somewhere*:

> *The last child appeared as the school bell stopped ringing, dawdling as much as he dared.*

Edge

To move in a certain direction very cautiously, *step by step and with great care*, especially when there is danger:

> *Terrified of being seen and challenged, she edged along in the shadow of the wall.*

Flounce (mostly with "out of")

To leave a place *in great indignation*, which shows by the way you do it. (Women are much better than men at this!):

> *"You beast!" she exclaimed, and flounced out indignantly.*

Hobble

To walk *as if it hurts to put each foot to the ground*, as happens to people with sore feet. Hobbling may also occur when the feet are fastened together or clothing round the ankles prevents normal walking:

The old woman hobbled painfully to the door, complaining of her corns.

They hobble the hind legs of their horses when they're not riding to prevent them wandering off.

Lag (usually with "behind")

To walk *more slowly* than the other people with you. (One who does this is called a **laggard,** although other terms also exist):

Come on, you slowcoaches! Stop lagging, or we'll never get there!

Limp

To walk unevenly, *leaning more heavily on one foot* than on the other, perhaps because you have hurt your foot or because one leg is shorter than the other is:

It was only a tiny stone in my shoe, but it kept me limping all the rest of the way.

Linger

This is really a negative action: you *don't go somewhere*, trying not to leave the place where you are, because you are fascinated by something there:

The girls kept lingering at every clothing shop, and we all got fed up with waiting for them.

March

As this verb is typical of the military, we use it to describe the energetic walk of *someone who is indignant and ready for conflict*:

The door flew open and Henry marched across the hall and into the manager's office, obviously furious about something.

Mince

To walk with *affected or exaggerated* delicacy and daintiness:

We were amused at the way the waiter minced out, head up and carrying his tray as though it were a bouquet of flowers.

Pace

To walk with *equal steps*, perhaps to measure the length of something or perhaps – especially when it is a to-and-fro movement – because you are deep in thought. A caged animal is likely to do this out of sheer boredom:

The prisoner knew exactly how long his cell was – he had paced it daily for the last year.

Pad

If you are *wearing very soft footwear*, it muffles your footsteps, so padding represents more the sound than a particular way of walking:

Soundless in his soft footwear, the old Chinese padded in and out quite unobtrusively.

Plod

To walk *steadily but putting all your weight on each foot in turn*. People usually do this when they are very tired but have to arrive somewhere:

We passed groups of farm labourers plodding doggedly homewards at the end of their long day.

Prowl

This is typical of beasts of prey: an animal that is waiting for an opportunity to attack *walks slowly round*, just out of reach:

The camp is always ringed with thorn-bushes at night because there is so often a lion or two prowling round, seeking a chance to attack the cattle.

Ramble

This is a gentle kind of sport in which a group of people set off *to walk, usually in the country, for pleasure*. There is often no precise destination and the route chosen mostly depends on the beauty of the surroundings:

At weekends they generally go rambling with their friends, no matter what the weather, and they always end up in a pub!

Saunter

To walk rather slowly in the circumstances, either because you are really totally relaxed or because you *want to give that impression*. This may be because you are really very uneasy but want to hide the fact. (Compare with **stroll**):

> *Watched by the rest of the class, Bill sauntered along the corridor to the headmaster's room, but he pulled his hands out of his pockets when he got to the door.*

Shuffle

To go slowly, *pushing your feet forward without lifting them off the ground* and thus making a characteristic noise with each step. We associate this behaviour with the very old or with people who are intensely unhappy, such as prisoners:

> *We could hear him shuffling about inside, but he didn't come and open the door when we knocked.*

Sidle   (usually with "into" or "out of")

To *move sideways* as unobtrusively as you can, because you want to avoid being noticed:

> *Towards the end of the lecture, students at the back began to sidle along the rows and out of the hall.*

Slip   (usually with "into" or "out of")

To go somewhere quickly, *knowing that the action will not take long*:

> *Wait a couple of minutes, will you, while I slip into the post office and post this letter.*

Stagger

To proceed very uncertainly, sometimes stopping and often on the point of falling. This describes the walk of someone who is *drunk, dizzy, very weak, or carrying a very heavy burden*:

> *Sailors on the spree staggered tipsily out of the tavern, with a girl on either arm.*

> *From the footprints, this man was carrying something heavy; look how he was staggering.*

Steal   (usually with "into" or "out of")

To move *as quickly as you can but silently* – in order not to be seen or heard. (The more familiar sense of *taking something that is not yours* is derived from this verb.):

> *Seeing that her charge had fallen asleep, the nurse closed her book and stole out of the room.*

Step

To concentrate on the movement, putting *each foot down in turn, deliberately or carefully.* We do this when the ground is unsafe or when we are dancing:

> *Step cautiously here – it's marshy underfoot and you might sink in!*

Stride

To walk *purposefully (quickly and with long steps),* because you know where you are going and have a clear idea of what you want to do. Children and people with short legs cannot do this:

> *I see him every morning about this time, striding to the station as if he's going to reorganize the entire railway system.*

Stroll

To walk slowly because there is no hurry and you are *enjoying the activity, the company, or the surroundings:*

> *It was a gorgeous evening and they strolled home, chatting about the forthcoming party.*

Strut

To walk with *stiff, unbending legs,* as if you are very proud of your position or of some accomplishment:

> *The colonel strutted the bridge his men had built, admiring its lines and its strength.*

Swagger

To walk deliberately slowly, pushing your chest out or swinging your shoulders excessively. This is characteristic of *men who want to parade their masculinity or to attract attention* for some such reason:

Very conscious of the effect they were making on the local girls, the parading troops swaggered into the main square.

Tiptoe

As the formation of this word implies, a tiptoer tries to walk *without putting his heels to the ground*, usually to avoid making a noise, but sometimes to minimize contact with the surface:

I had only just washed the floor, so I had to tiptoe across it to get to the telephone.

Toddle

This is the characteristic way of walking of people *with unusually short legs*, such as little children:

The acrobats were followed by several dwarfs, toddling behind them as fast as they could.

Traipse

You traipse when *you have to go to one place after another* (as when doing the daily shopping, perhaps) and are getting very tired but have to keep on in order to finish what you started:

We spent the whole morning traipsing from shop to shop, but we still couldn't find where she had left her bag.

Trot

Horses sometimes do this – walk with short steps and (in the case of a person) so quickly that you are *almost running*:

The train was due out at any moment, so she trotted anxiously along the platform, looking for an empty seat.

Trudge

This is similar to **traipse** in that you are tired and have to keep on. The difference here is that you have *only one destination, and persistence is the only way to get there*:

Despite his tiredness, he insisted on trudging home rather than accept a lift.

Waddle

To roll from side to side when walking. This verb is used mainly for the walk of ducks, but it can be effective to describe the walk of *a very fat and heavy person*:

> *The opera's heroine was supposed to be slim and lightfooted, but the part was played by a soprano so obese that she could only waddle grotesquely across the stage.*

Wade

To walk *through water* or a similar liquid:

> *In Roman times the Thames was shallow enough to be waded across at this point, and that's where the ford was.*

(Also see **Wander**)

122 WALL ~ FENCE ~ HEDGE ~ RAILING(S)

Wall

A **wall** is normally built of stone, or certain versions of stone such as brick or cement, although it is quite possible to have walls of metal, glass, rock, ice, etc. The essence of wall construction is that a wall is a solid object that can be penetrated only by means of a door or gate.

Fence

A **fence** is porous (it is no barrier to wind), since it is made of many connected parts so that people – or large animals – can see but cannot pass between these. Fences are made mostly of wood, but there are also wire fences.

Hedges

They are simply lines of tough bushes, planted so close together that it is very difficult to see through and impossible to penetrate without breaking the branches.

Railing(s)

They are lines of slim vertical metal rods (held together by transverse pieces) that enable one to see through easily, as the purpose is defence rather than privacy. They are used principally as a protection round or outside important buildings, or round public parks and gardens.

123 WANDER ~ ROAM ~ ROVE ~ STRAY

All of these are verbs, although some are nouns too, and in every case the movement is slow or leisurely and mostly made without a clear destination in mind.

Wander

This verb has these characteristics:

1. It sometimes shows walking in an *unintended direction*:

    She realised that in her abstraction she had wandered into an unfamiliar part of the palace.

2. It often means *illness*, especially *dizziness*:

    The falling branch had struck him so hard that he was found wandering and semi-conscious in the park.

3. It can mean that someone is *lost*:

    I wandered about for hours before I found a street I recognized, and then I knew where I was.

4. We can use it to describe a way of *walking without aim*, perhaps for pleasure or relaxation:

    After dinner we went out and wandered through the old part of the city, which we found fascinating.

Roam

This can be done either on foot or by any other means and there is often *no particular purpose* in the act:

We roamed the old streets of the town for over an hour, enjoying the festive atmosphere.

Rove

(This is a rather romantic verb, not much used in modern English). *Long periods and distances* are implied, and the movement is both *relaxed and purposeless*:

He spent many years roving the world and gaining experience of life.

Stray

This is always accidental: the person (especially a child or, very often, an animal) goes the wrong way and, as can happen with **wander**, *ends up in an unintended place*:

A cow had strayed into our garden and was eating Father's cabbages ...!

From the lost way he's running about, that dog looks like a stray to me.

124 WANT ~ WISH ~ DESIRE

Want

In its commonest sense (when it is followed by an infinitive) this verb expresses a very elementary feeling: an urge to do something specific, either at once or in the near future:

Come here: I want to show you something.

Well, do you want to eat it or not?

They didn't want to see us again.

Used with a direct object and no second verb, it signifies a need or an urge for possession:

It's your money he wants, not your devotion!

Who wants this last piece of cake?

In speaking angrily about another person, and also when used with a gerund, however, the meaning is *need*:

That child wants (= needs) a good smack!

Your glasses want cleaning rather badly, don't they?

This piece of work looks good at first sight, but it really wants careful revising to be fully acceptable.

Wish

It is another way of expressing **want**, when used with an infinitive. But it is used in formal situations only, or its use makes the statement sound very formal – sometimes pompous, in fact:

Application letter: I wish to apply for the post of...

Lawyer in court: My client wishes to make it clear that...

Haughty secretary: Did you wish (instead of "Do you want") to see Mr Everett?

Desire

Used with a direct object, this is often employed to show lust or passion, especially in describing historical settings:

Sheherezade's long tales at night-time entertained the sultan too much to want to cut them short and kept him desiring her.

Used with an infinitive, it becomes another very formal and unfriendly way of expressing **want**:

"Do you desire us to replace the garment, then, madam?" asked the shop manager icily.

125 WILLING ~ PREPARED ~ READY ~ KEEN ~ EAGER

All these adjectives show that someone will do something if it is required, but the degree of enthusiasm varies.

Willing and Prepared

These, surprisingly, are the least strong. The implication is that the person *will do what is wanted, but only if asked, or because he has already been asked.* He is unlikely to volunteer to do it. These two adjectives are the most used in asking questions, when the speaker cannot be at all sure of the response, and of these **prepared** is the more likely in negative sentences:

Are you willing / prepared to give up so much for my sake?

He said he was willing / prepared to lend us a hand if need be, but it was pretty clear that he would prefer not to!

I am certainly not prepared to answer any questions unless my lawyer is present.

Ready

This shows a more positive attitude: the person has made all the preparations and now is only *waiting* – and very likely expecting – *to be asked*:

Mrs Allen was already sitting at the piano, ready to start playing as soon as she was asked to.

I like that new girl in the office; she always has such a ready smile for everyone.
She smiles at people whenever she has an opportunity.

I wasn't quite ready for a photograph just then and so I had this silly expression of surprise on my face.

Keen

It is stronger still. He clearly either very much enjoys what he is doing already or *looks forward to doing what is wanted* and will do it with pleasure when the moment comes:

My son is a keen golfer; he never misses a game if he can avoid it.

After several days of waiting, the troops were keen to see some action, and when at last they were given the order to attack they rose to it as one man.

Eager

It is the strongest of all. Here the person wants to do something so much that *he can hardly wait*:

The children were all so eager to be first to the top of the slide that poor little Winnie got pushed off and sprained her ankle.

The race started with much eager jostling for position, but after a few minutes impatience gave way to determination as the runners' energy began to wane.

126 WORTH ~ WORTH WHILE ~ WORTHWHILE ~ WORTHY

Worth (a noun, meaning *value* or *importance*.

Used with "to be", as in "**It's worth** (a certain amount)", it shows *the value ascribed to something*:

> *The old book was found to be worth a fortune.*

When followed by a gerund, as in "**It wasn't worth** going back", it is *the result (known or expected) of some special effort*:

> *Do you think it's worth trying again?*
> Do you think the effort or trouble of trying again will have a reasonable result?

Remember the phrase "for all (my, his, etc.) worth", which means *making the greatest effort possible* to do something:

> *We saw them running for all their worth towards the station.*

Worth while (two separate words and also used with "to be")

As the word **while** simply means *effort*, a phrase like "**It'll be worth while**" means *It'll be worth making the (necessary) effort*:

> *I thought of demanding an apology, but I realized that it wasn't worth while.*

It is possible to personalize this kind of case by inserting a possessive adjective (my, your, his, etc.) before **while**:

> *It wouldn't have been worth your while to make a fuss.*

Worthwhile (one word)

This adjective has the meaning of *useful* or *valuable*:

> *She's doing a very worthwhile job as a Red Cross nurse.*

Worthy

Here is another adjective, used for people or their work, with the meaning of *admirable, respected,* or *valuable to the community*:

He made a worthy (= admirable) attempt to smile when he lost the game.

The traditional interpretation of the Bow bells chime in London is: "Turn again, Whittington, thou worthy citizen".

Its negative form, **unworthy**, means *ignoble* or *too poor to be considered*:

It would be unworthy of you to back out now.

The Editor rejected his report as being unworthy of mention.

127 WRECK ~ WRECKAGE ~ SHIPWRECK

Wreck

This is what is left of vehicles of transport (ships, planes, trains, buses, cars, etc.) after a disaster such as a sinking (in the case of a ship) or a crash (in the case of airborne or land vehicles). The **wreck** is more or less whole and is still recognizable but is *too badly damaged to be used any more*. This term is also used metaphorically to describe the ruin of some kind of enterprise or of somebody's life:

The wreck of the Titanic has been located, but it is so large and is at so great a depth that raising it is out of the question as yet.

They are trying to save something from the wreck of the company, but little can be done unless the government agrees to underwrite the cost.

Wreckage

When a transport vehicle (or possibly a building) suffers some kind of explosion or violent impact it *breaks into many parts*, which are found scattered over a wide area. These parts constitute the **wreckage**:

The aircraft had hit the mountainside with such force that the wreckage had been flung about for over a mile in all directions.

Shipwreck

This is the abstract term used to describe the accident of the sinking, destruction, or loss of a ship, almost always at sea:

Insurance companies may have to pay out tremendous amounts in compensation in the event of catastrophes such as shipwreck, earthquakes, or oil-spills.

INDEX

This alphabetic index includes all the words or phrases given specifically in this book. Each word quoted here is followed by a second word or phrase in parenthesis and printed in **bold** letters, which refers to the "Contents: List of Problem Items" (also in alphabetic order) at the beginning of the book, indicating where you can find it. For example, "Abduct" is followed by (**Taking**), which means that to find it in the list of Problem Items, you must look under "**Taking**". In some cases, the same word is listed under two Problem Items.

Cremate (**Burning**)
Cringe (**Duck**)
Crouch (**Posture**)
Cry, cry out (**Loudness of voice**)
D
Dart (**Running**)
Dash (**Running**)
Dawdle (**Walking**)
Dazzle (**Light**)
Deal (**Unexpected Applications**)
Deadly (**Fatal**)
Deathly (**Fatal**)
Debate (**Argument**)
Deliver (**Unexpected Applications**)
Denude (**Bare**) (verb)
Desire (verb) (**Want**)
Desperation (**Despair**)
Detect (**Find**)
Differentiate (**Differ**)
Discern (**Seeing**)
Discover (**Find**)
Discussion (**Argument**)
Dishonest (**Sincere**)
Dissuade (**Convince**)
Distinguish (**Differ**) (**Seeing**)
Disturb (**Annoy**)
Doorway (**Door**)
Doubtless (**Undoubtedly**)
Drag (**Pulling**)
Draw (**Pulling**) (**Unexpected Applications**)
Drip (**Liquids**)
Drive (**Pushing**)
E
Eager (**Willing**)
East (**North**)
Easterly (**North**)
Eastern (**North**)
Edge (verb) (**Walking**)

Electric, electrical (**-ic / -ical Endings**)
Embezzle (**Taking**)
Encounter (**Find**)
Entertaining (**Amusing**)
Entry (**Entrance**)
Especial, especially (**Special**)
Evident (**Obvious**)
Exchange (**Change**)
Expect (**Wait**)
Expose (**Bare**) (verb)
Expound (**Bare**) (verb)
Eye (verb) (**Looking**)
F
Fame (**Famous**)
Fast (**Quick**)
Fence (**Wall**)
Filch (**Taking**)
Filthy (**Dirty**)
Final (**Last**)
Finish (**End**)
Fire (**Shoot**)
Flare (**Light**)
Flash (**Light**)
Flicker (**Light**)
Flood (**Liquids**)
Floodlight (**Light**)
Flounce (**Walking**)
Flow (**Liquids**)
Form (**Shape**)
Foul (**Dirty**)
Frank (**Sincere**)
Frisk (**Running**)
Frontier (**Border**)
Frown (**Looking**)
Full (**Plenty**)
Fun, funny (**Amusing**)
G
Gain (**Earn**)
Gallop (**Running**)
Gambol (**Running**)

Game (**Unexpected Applications**)
Gash (**Cutting**)
Gate (**Door**)
Gateway (**Door**)
Gawp (**Looking**)
Gaze (**Looking**)
Giggle (**Laughing**)
Gilded (**Golden**)
Gilt (**Golden**)
Give (**Unexpected Applications**)
Glad (**Happy**)
Glance (**Looking**)
Glare (**Looking**)
Gleam (**Light**)
Glimmer (**Light**)
Glimpse (**Seeing**)
Glint (**Light**)
Glisten (**Light**)
Glitter (**Light**)
Gloss (**Light**)
Glow (**Light**)
Glower (**Looking**)
Goad (**Pushing**)
Goggle (**Looking**)
Gouge (**Cutting**)
Grand (**Big**)
Gratified (**Grateful**)
Gratitude (**Grateful**)
Great, greater (**Big**)
Grimy (**Dirty**)
Grin (**Laughing**)
Grip (**Holding**)
Ground (**Earth**)
Grovel (**Duck**)
Grubby (**Dirty**)
Guffaw (**Laughing**)
Gush (**Liquids**)
H
Hack (**Cutting**)
Hamlet (**City**)

Harbour (**Port**)
Haul (**Pulling**)
Haven (**Port**)
Heave (**Pushing**)
Hedge (**Wall**)
Height (**Tall**)
High (**Tall**)
Hijack (**Taking**)
Hire (**Rent**)
Hit (**Shoot**)
Hobble (**Walking**)
Hoist (**Pulling**)
Hold (**Unexpected Applications**)
Honest (**Sincere**)
Hop (**Running**)
Hope (**Wait**)
Huddle (**Posture**)
Hustle (**Pushing**)

I
Ignite (**Burning**)
Illuminate (**Light**)
I'm sure (**Undoubtedly**)
Impel (**Pushing**)
Imply (**Hint**)
Incinerate (**Burning**)
Incise (**Cutting**)
Inform (**Unexpected Applications**)
Insincere (**Sincere**)
Insinuate (**Hint**)
Interchange (**Change**)
Intimacy (**Private**)
Intimate (**Private**) (**Hint**)
Intimation (**Private**)
Issue (**Matter**)

J
Jeer (**Scoff**)
Jog (**Pushing**)
Jostle (**Pushing**)
Jumping (**Running**)

K
Keen (**Willing**)

Kidnap (**Taking**)
Killer (**Assassin**)

L
Lag (**Walking**)
Laggard (**Walking**)
Land (**Earth**)
Landscape (**Town**)
Large (**Big**)
Latest (**Last**)
Launch (**Pushing**)
Lead (**Golden**)
Leaden (**Golden**)
Lean (**Posture**)
Leap (**Running**)
Lease (**Rent**)
Leer (**Looking**)
Lethal (**Fatal**)
Lie (**Lay**)
Limp (**Walking**)
Linger (**Walking**)
Livelihood (**Life**)
Living (noun) (**Life**)
Locate (**Find**)
Loll (**Posture**)
Loot (**Taking**)
Lop (**Cutting**)
Lope (**Running**)
Low (**Tall**)
Lug (**Pulling**)
Lustre (**Light**)

M
Magic, magical (**-ic/-ical Endings**)
Malicious (**Mischievous**)
Manner (**View**)
March (**Walking**)
Market town (**City**)
Meet (**Find**) (**Unexpected Applications**)
Meet with (**Find**)
Mince (**Walking**)
Misappropriate (**Taking**)
Miss (**Shoot**)

Mock (**Scoff**)
Mortal (**Fatal**)
Molest (**Annoy**)
Mug (verb) (**Taking**)
Murder (**Assassin**)
Murderer (**Assassin**)

N
Naked (**Bare**)
Nearly (**Almost**)
Nick (verb) (**Cutting**)
No doubt (**Undoubtedly**)
Notice (verb) (**Realize**) (**Seeing**)
Notoriety (**Famous**)
Notorious (**Famous**)
Nude (**Bare**)
Nudge (**Pushing**)
Nuisance (**Trouble**)

O
Obtain (**Reach**)
Ogle (**Looking**)
Only (**Just, Only**)
Ooze (**Liquids**)
Opinion (**View**)
Opportunity (**Occasion**)
Optimist, optimistic (**-ic/-ical Endings**)
Outlook (**View**)
Over (**Above**)

P
Pace (**Walking**)
Pad (**Walking**)
Pare (**Cutting**)
Patent (**Obvious**)
Peel (**Cutting**)
Peep (**Looking**)
Peer (**Looking**)
Perceive (**Seeing**)
Personality (**Character**)
Persuade (**Convince**)
Pest (**Plague**)
Pilfer (**Taking**)
Pitiful (**Sympathy**)

Pity (**Sympathy**)
Plagiarize (**Taking**)
Pleased (**Happy**)
Plod (**Walking**)
Plunder (**Taking**)
Poach (**Taking**)
Point of view (**View**)
Poke (**Pushing**)
Politic, political (**-ic/-ical Endings**)
Pollute (**Contaminate**)
Pop (verb) (**Running**)
Pounce (**Running**)
Pour (**Liquids**)
Prepared (**Willing**)
Press (**Pushing**)
Prevent (**Avoid**)
Problem (**Matter**)
Prod (**Pushing**)
Produce (**Product**)
Propel (**Pushing**)
Prospect (**Aspect**)
Prove (**Control**)
Prowl (**Walking**)
Prune (**Cutting**)
Purloin (**Taking**)

Q
Quickly (**Soon**)

R
Race (verb) (**Running**)
Railing(s) (**Wall**)
Ramble (**Walking**)
Rapid (**Quick**)
Ready (**Willing**)
Regard (**Looking**)
Replace (**Substitute**)
Reveal (**Bare**) (verb)
Roadway (**Road**)
Roam (**Wander**)
Rove (**Wander**)
Run (**Liquids**)
Run into (**Find**)
Rustle (**Taking**)

S
Sack (verb) (**Taking**)
Sad (**Happy**)
Safe (**Sure**)
Saunter (**Walking**)
Saw (verb) (**Cutting**)
Scald (**Burning**)
Scamper (**Running**)
Scan (**Looking**)
Scintillate (**Light**)
Scorch (**Burning**)
Score (verb) (**Cutting**)
Scowl (**Looking**)
Scramble (**Running**)
Scratch (**Cutting**)
Scream (**Loudness of voice**)
Screech (**Loudness of voice**)
Scrutinize (**Looking**)
Scuttle (**Running**)
Sear (**Burning**)
Seaside (**Beach**)
Secure (**Sure**)
Seep (**Liquids**)
Set light, set fire to (**Burning**)
Sever (**Cutting**)
Shave (**Cutting**)
Shear (**Cutting**)
Sheen (**Light**)
Sheer (**Full**)
Shimmer (**Light**)
Shine (**Light**)
Shipwreck (**Wreck**)
Shoot (**Running**)
(**Unexpected Applications**)
Shoplift (**Taking**)
Shore (**Beach**)
Short (**Tall**)
Short-change (**Taking**)
Shout (**Loudness of voice**)
Shove (**Pushing**)
Shriek (**Loudness of voice**)
Shuffle (**Walking**)

Sidle (**Walking**)
Sight (noun) (**Aspect**)
Sight (verb) (**Seeing**)
Signal (**Sign**)
Silver (**Golden**)
Silvery (**Golden**)
Simper (**Laughing**)
Singe (**Burning**)
Skip (**Running**)
Slash (**Cutting**)
Slice (**Cutting**)
Slip (**Walking**)
Slit (**Cutting**)
Slop (**Liquids**)
Small (**Little**)
Smiling (**Laughing**)
Smirk (**Laughing**)
Smoulder (**Burning**)
Snigger (**Laughing**)
Snip (**Cutting**)
Soil (**Earth**)
South (**North**)
Southerly (**North**)
Southern (**North**)
Sparkle (**Light**)
Spatter (**Liquids**)
Spill (**Liquids**)
Spiteful (**Mischievous**)
Splash (**Liquids**)
Spot (verb) (**Seeing**)
Spout (**Liquids**)
Sprawl (**Posture**)
Spray (**Liquids**)
Spring (verb) (**Running**)
Spurt (**Liquids**)
Spy (verb) (**Seeing**)
Squat (**Posture**)
Squeal (**Loudness of voice**)
Squint (**Looking**)
Squirt (**Liquids**)
Stagger (**Walking**)
Stare (**Looking**)
Start (**Begin**)

Start to / Start –ing (**Begin to**)
Steal (**Rob**) (**Walking**)
Step (**Walking**)
Stoop (**Posture**)
Storey (**Floor**)
Strand (**Beach**)
Stray (**Wander**)
Stream (verb) (**Liquids**)
Street (**Road**)
Stride (**Walking**)
Stroll (**Walking**)
Strut (**Walking**)
Stub (**Pushing**)
Subject (**Matter**)
Suit (**Fit**)
Survey (verb) (**Looking**)
Swagger (**Walking**)
Swift (**Quick**)
Swindle (**Taking**)
Swirl (**Liquids**)
Switch (verb) (**Change**)
Sympathetic (**Sympathy**)
Sympathize (**Sympathy**)
T
Taunt (**Scoff**)
Tease (**Scoff**)
Tell, telling (**Unexpected Applications**)
Test (**Control**)
Thankful, thankless (**Grateful**)
The two (**Both**)
Theme (**Matter**)
Thieve (**Taking**)
Thrust (**Pushing**)

Tiptoe (**Walking**)
Titter (**Laughing**)
Toddle (**Walking**)
Topic (**Matter**)
Tow (**Pulling**)
Town (**City**)
Trail (verb) (**Pulling**)
Traipse (**Walking**)
Trickle (**Liquids**)
Trim (**Cutting**)
Trot (**Walking**)
Troublesome (**Trouble**)
Trudge (**Walking**)
Truthful (**Sincere**)
Try (**Control**) (**Unexpected Applications**)
Try out (**Control**)
Trying (**Unexpected Applications**)
Tug (**Pulling**)
Twinkle (**Light**)
U
Ultimate (**Last**)
Uncover (**Bare**) (verb)
Under, underneath (**Above**)
Unearth (**Bare**) (verb)
Unhappy (**Happy**)
Untruthful (**Sincere**)
Unworthy (**Worth**)
Utter (**Full**)
V
Variety (**Differ**)
Vary (**Differ**)
Vault (verb) (**Running**)
Vessel (**Ship**)
View (verb) (**Looking**)

Viewpoint (**View**)
Vicious (**Mischievous**)
Village (**City**)
W
Waddle (**Walking**)
Wade (**Walking**)
Wall (**Door**)
Watch (verb) (**Looking**)
Well (**Liquids**)
West (**North**)
Westerly (**North**)
Western (**North**)
Whittle (**Cutting**)
Win (**Earn**)
Wish (**Want**)
Without doubt (**Undoubtedly**)
Witness (**Seeing**)
Wood (**Golden**)
Wooden (**Golden**)
Wool (**Golden**)
Woollen (**Golden**)
Work (**Unexpected Applications**)
Worthwhile (**Worth**)
Worthy (**Worth**)
Worry (**Annoy**) (**Preoccupy**)
Wreckage (**Wreck**)
Y
Yell (**Loudness of voice**)

THE AUTHOR

Peter Rutherford is a native Londoner who holds the Royal Society of Arts Diploma for teaching English as a Foreign Language.

At the age of twenty-five he left Britain and for a number of years taught English in Germany. Then he settled permanently in Spain, working for many years as a teacher at the British Council Institute in Madrid, where he specialized in preparing candidates for the Proficiency examinations of the University of Cambridge.

For most of that time he has also been an officially appointed local oral examiner for that same university, at both First Certificate and Proficiency levels.

FROM THE SAME PUBLISHER

GRAMMAR & REFERENCE BOOKS

El inglés compendiado. An Easy English Grammar. Manual de gramática inglesa muy completo, claro, práctico y esquemático. La obra es una recopilación de normas gramaticales que sirven tanto para repasar la mecánica del idioma o conceptos ya estudiados, como para sacar de dudas al estudioso en un momento concreto. El libro está dividido en 20 temas o capítulos, cada uno dedicado a un punto gramatical, pensado y diseñado especialmente para hispanohablantes.

Las preposiciones inglesas y sus ejercicios. La información recopilada en este libro no se encuentra como tal en ningún tratado de gramática. Abundantes frases prácticas, 35 ejercicios y soluciones.

La palabra justa en inglés. Choose your Words Carefully. Se comparan pares de palabras básicas, como Do-Make; Say-Tell, hasta un total de 50 grupos, explicando su uso correcto. Abundantes ejercicios con su clave.

Las dificultades idiomáticas del inglés. Resuelve de manera muy práctica las dificultades que se presentan con mayor frecuencia.

To Get. El verbo comodín del inglés. Estudio completo y sumamente práctico de este verbo. Con 25 ejercicios y soluciones.

EXERCISES & TESTS IN ENGLISH

100 tests para reavivar su inglés. Selección de 100 Tests muy variados, divididos en tres niveles: elemental, intermedio y avanzado. Con soluciones.

Inglés en acción. Prácticas de vocabulario. Contiene 400 ejercicios para practicar vocabulario de palabras inglesas de forma amena y divertida. Incluye un pequeño diccionario para consulta. Con soluciones. Nivel intermedio.

Ejercicios de verbos ingleses combinados con partículas. (Phrasal & Prepositional Verbs). Más de 1.000 ejercicios sobre estos verbos, con soluciones. Complemento de: "Verbos ingleses combinados con partículas" de la misma editorial.

Cuaderno de ejercicios en inglés. Práctica de gramática y estructuras. Variadísimos ejercicios para repasar la gramática inglesa. Por su estructura y vocabulario puede usarse acompañando a cualquier método de inglés existente en el mercado. Está estructurado por temas a fin de practicar todos los puntos gramaticales. Contiene 140 ejercicios con soluciones. (Complemento del libro "El inglés compendiado. An easy English grammar" de la misma editorial.

PRACTICE IN TRANSLATION SPANISH-ENGLISH.

Textos literarios para traducir. Español-inglés. Nivel avanzado. Textos literarios de autores contemporáneos de habla española traducidos al inglés con numerosas notas y variantes alternativas. Muy útil para alumnos avanzados y opositores.

Cuaderno para la traducción inversa. Español-inglés. Verbos. Contiene 165 ejercicios de traducción inversa (español-inglés) sobre verbos corrientes pero que presentan una cierta dificultad para el estudiante español. Unico por las alternativas a todas las traducciones.

SPECIALIZED DICTIONARIES

Catálogo de expresiones para la traducción inversa. Español - inglés. Más de 7.000 expresiones de uso corriente que facilitan tanto la expresión oral como escrita.

Diccionario auxiliar del traductor. Español-inglés. The Translator's Auxiliary Dictionary. Más de 5.000 frases de uso corriente para ilustrar el uso de las palabras del lenguaje cotidiano.

English False Friends. Palabras inglesas engañosas. Selección de palabras inglesas cuyo parecido con otras españolas es motivo de equivocaciones. Con ejercicios y soluciones.

The English Tom, Dick & Harry Speak. Español - inglés. Esta obra recoge una selección de 3.000 modismos, dichos, expresiones coloquiales y frases de sentido figurado, denominados idioms en inglés. Imprescindible para comunicarse en situaciones coloquiales. Nivel avanzado.

English Slang. Inglés - Español. Contiene más de 2.000 expresiones de slang en inglés moderno. Es una gran ayuda para entender el idioma que se oye en la calle, y a veces, en televisión y que incluso se puede ver impreso en los periódicos ingleses más populares. Nivel avanzado.

Diccionario de dudas del inglés. Diccionario excepcional que analiza y resuelve las dudas del estudiante español. Esta obra ha recibido el Premio de Lexicografía Bilingüe en el II Certamen de Lexicografía Bilingüe que se celebró en 1996 en la Universidad de Extremadura (España).

Diccionario de verbos ingleses. Enfoque novedoso. Estudio de los verbos con relación a los diferentes elementos que les siguen, como son: preposiciones, objeto directo e indirecto, infinitivo con o sin "to", los llamados "gerunds", así como participios presentes o pasados. Nivel avanzado.

Diccionario de frases inglesas. Diccionario de palabras inglesas que tienen varias acepciones en español. Más de 3.500 frases ilustrativas. Esta obra pretende ser un instrumento de comunicación al presentar las palabras de forma activa, empleadas en un contexto, lo que facilita la comprensión y muestra el uso de cada una. Nivel intermedio.

ENGLISH PRONUNCIATION BOOKS

La pronunciación inglesa. Fonética y fonología. Estudio práctico de los sonidos ingleses. Ilustrado con 50 dibujos y 10 fotos. Con cassette.

Ejercicios de transcripción fonética en inglés. 45 párrafos graduados para practicar la transcripción fonética. Desde la frase al texto. Con notas y soluciones.

Práctica de pronunciación inglesa. English Pronunciation Practice. Contiene 75 ejercicios de entrenamiento auditivo. Con soluciones y transcripción fonética de las palabras.

Fonética funcional inglesa. Manual muy completo y práctico de pronunciación inglesa. Estudio de los sonidos, la acentuación de las palabras, ritmo y entonación. Con ejercicios.

Catálogo Gratuito

Solicite de forma gratuita nuestro catálogo completo y totalmente actualizado de Libros Didácticos Complementarios escribiendo a la siguiente dirección, o llamando al teléfono que se indica.

Anglo-Didáctica Publishing
C/ Santiago de Compostela, 16 – bajo B
28034 Madrid
Tel y Fax: 91 378 01 88